Culture Shock - My Cuban Refugee Family in South Dakota

Front: L-R: Cuban Juana Perez + Dr. Philip Stack + Cuban Maria Perez Dela Cruz + Cuban Geronimo Dela Cruz. . . . .At back: Dra. Fe Stack

Soley Gonzales, subsequently born in USA to this Cuban refugee family

The True Story of A Cuban Refugee Family In South Dakota

By Dr. Philip Stack
Spring Hill, Tennessee

Dr. Philip L. Stack is a Pennsylvanian by birth and the son of refugee parents. He is a resident of Tabor, South Dakota. As a Psychologist, he considers the intact, happy family as a crucial part of society. He offers marriage counseling and family therapy and has written How to do Family Therapy, a book for married couples. He and his wife, Fe, are parents of one girl and five boys. The Stacks have had the challenging experience of living with five teen agers under the same roof.
The author was Cub Master for 10 years and in 1976 the Stack family was honored by the Boy Scouts of America with a Family of the year Award.
In his philosophy Dr. Stack offers a simple guideline: a person should be good to his family, to his country and to the world in his lifetime.

STATE OF SOUTH DAKOTA
EXECUTIVE OFFICE
WILLIAM J. JANKLOW
GOVERNOR

FOREWORD

When the federal government called the State of South Dakota in the spring of 1980 to see if we could offer temporary housing for a small number of the many thousand Cuban refugees who were coming to America, I said that South Dakotans would be glad to help.

Unfortunately, the darker side of human nature appeared and many South Dakotans voiced their outrage at my willingness to offer help to those who were fleeing from communist tyranny and oppression. I reluctantly told the federal government that none of our empty dormitories or barracks could be used that summer for temporary housing while the refugees were being processed and selected for homes.

Although a minority, many South Dakotans did support efforts to help the refugees. A few families stepped forward and voluntarily offered their homes as places for settlement. These families realized that the ideals and principals that lead to the founding of the United States should not be abandoned in the twentieth century because they might cause inconvenience. They realized that most Americans and most South Dakotans were either boat people chemselves or the descendants of boat people. They realized that they would not have the life they have today without the kindness and generosity that was either given to them or their ancestors.

Such a family of caring South Dakotans is the Philip Stack family of Tabor. When they saw that thousands were in need, they decided to help—not just with a contribution of money or nice words of support. They offered their homes and themselves as sponsors of a Cuban refugee family.

What follows is a diary of the Stack family's life with Geronimo, Maria and Juana—husband, wife and mother-in-law. Although the obvious story of the new Americans' adjustment to an entirely, new social system is amusing, poignant and thought- provoking at many times, the diary is much more than that. It is also a chronicle of the real-life problems that are felt and faced by human beings in every culture and society.

Throughout the reading of the diary, I could not help but wonder how I would have reacted to every new surprising situation. I wondered what my family would have done. The surprise ending also makes me hope that there will be sequel.

This diary is much more interesting than any imagined story, television drama or motion picture. It is a fascinating account of a family reaching across barriers of language, custom and culture to help another family in their pursuit of happiness and freedom. This real-life drama of two families deepened my admiration for the Stack family and made me feel happy that the best of human nature can also come forward in people and dominate a situation so that great good can be done.

Sincerely yours,

William J. Janklow
WJJ:jj

Dedication

This book is dedicated with honor to the fifteen year old Chinese youth who fled Communist China leaving his family behind, to the Vietnamese family who endured the perils of drowning as they sought freedom in America, to the Pole who remains apprehensive about discussing freedom because he calls it a "political issue" and after 15 years, feels he must protect his family in Poland, to the Irishman who fled the Potato Famine and came to the Land of Opportunity, to the Jew who lost his first family to Hitler and gratefully began his second family in America, to Suzanna and Joseph Stack who came to Pennsylvania from Czechoslovakia in 1920 to find a better life for their children and to all boat people and their offspring and to all who helped them achieve happiness in a Great Land.

Publisher

Self-published & printed in USA by Tatay Jobo Elizes with Author's permission using Print-On-Demand System (POD) and Kindle Edition. Tatay Jobo Elizes is a Self-Publisher in USA. Published 2012 under the following ISBN numbers:
ISBN-13: 978- *1478241096*   ISBN-10: *1478241098*

Culture Shock
My Cuban Refugee Family in South Dakota

Friday, July 4 Perez and De La Cruz. Perez and De La Cruz: Three members of a Cuban family, one Perez and two De La Cruz.

Fort Chaffee called three times in the last two weeks, each caller offering a new Cuban family.

"I already have one," I told them, after hearing a litany of positive features about each.

I could tell they were desperate to find new sponsors.

Only bits of information seemed to reach me about my Cuban family. They were hard workers, deeply religious, well educated, two being college instructors.

It was practically time for the Cubans' arrival when I learned that one was pregnant, five months along.

Flight 977 would be arriving from Omaha at eight. We had 20 miles to travel and we could be late.

I scolded Amelia,, my wife, who delayed our departure from home because she wanted to change into her best suit.

We had but three minutes to spare as we drove in the gate of the West View Airport.

'Thank goodness," they would not land before we arrived. Our absence could be upsetting and very demoralizing to them.

The security officer greeted us at the door.

"I got bad news for you. The 977 is delayed in Omaha . . .mechanical failure."

Having reached the peak of our excitement, we felt very dis-appointed on hearing the news. Unfortunately, the next day Amelia would be working and. being Filipino, she did know a tiny bit of Spanish.

Saturday. July 5 This morning Amelia and I were up bright and early, arriving at the airport with fifteen minutes to spare.

We anxiously searched the southern sky for signs of the new flight. 953.

Dropping through the low-hanging clouds. it finally slid onto the runway.

The Cubans were the first to leave the plane, a sad-looking, weather-beaten lot, forlorn and frightened. Geronimo. Maria, and Juana: in that order they marched in single file.

Geronimo, over six feet tall, powerfully built, was the darkest, a coal black man with a protruding abdomen. He was 23 but looked 30.

Geronimo's wife, Maria, abdomen bulging, peered straight ahead, her slender neck stretching, like a giraffe's, for a reassuring view as the entered the terminal. She had a tan-like complexion with dark, kinky hair and one tooth missing in her lower jaw.

Her mother. Juana, with a stern, wrinkled face and sunken eyes earned the only piece of luggage, a small, broken nutcase. Her gait was awkward but agile, a bulging growth in her neck the size of a golf ball dangling with every step.

As we reached out to each other I could feel the overwhelming sense of ineptness and bungling within me.

What would it be like now that two cultures, two languages, two races, two countries, two traditions were merging?

Geronimo's handshake was especially flaccid and uninspiring.

Only then did I notice his deformed, left arm.

I never did get to try my "mi amigo" and my "mi amiga" on them which I had been practicing for this delicate moment.

After driving Amelia to her work at the hospital, I drove my three Cubans the final twenty miles to their next home. It was on the trail of Lewis and Clark, a small, isolated farm community in the Mid West, population, 400.

This was not a populous Havana, with its teeming tens of thousands. It was a quiet, restful community where the people knew each oilier intimately. It was a community which field high its own traditions and values.

Realistically, I anticipated that the infusion of the Cubans into the town's rural society would be unwelcomed by some.

Soon the gossiping, like a prairie fire, would pass through the town and reach into the country side.

I had prepared a suitable place for my three visitors, a furnished abode on main street that I sometimes used as a cafe. It served as a comfortable home for several families in the past.

In the rear was a large bedroom that I had furnished with two beds, one double and one single.

Amelia had purchased some bed spreads and pillow coven with a pretty cherry design and three new pillows for the new occupants.

The temperature outside was in thc 90s.

The air conditioning made it comfortable inside.

Still the Cubans could not communicate with me and I could not communicate with them. 1 felt particularly helpless when Juana reacted adversely to the proposed residence.

"House, no. House, no," she shouted repeatedly with her modicum of English.

Dissention between Geronimo and Juana suddenly erupted into a pocketbook-pulling contest. Geronimo wanted to be satisfied but the old lady persisted with her disenchantment.

Barefooted, she fled the building in a panic.

From one business place to another she dashed, her arms waving aimlessly in the air above her head, seeking some sort of respite from the strain she was feeling.

Like a drowning swimmer, her arms flailing, she half walked and half wobbled toward me as I watched her in dismay. With the hot asphalt on her bare feet she gasped, "no gusto, no gusto."

She didn't like it.

I had hoped it was only a temporary reaction as all three Cubans somehow settled down to a floor scrubbing and mopping.

Afterwards they wanted to rest, Geronimo asking about the mechanism for locking the rear door and whether the Ku Klux Klan were active in town.

Later I called Peter, a friend who received his college education in Mexico, and invited Maria to speak with him. She spoke quite rapidly and with considerable animation, then gave the phone to me.

"What's going on there? Everything is in turmoil. They don't like the place because there are insufficient facilities. They can't take a shower. t She's expecting a child and needs to see a doctor.

Maria's foot is sore and they have no clothes to wear.

What kind of place do you have them in anyway? They hate it."

I begged Peter to come soon so that we could understand each other better. He promised to come, "in a couple of hours."

Meanwhile, it was a seventeen room house I brought them to, only one block away. It was my home.

The mother and daughter exchanged some words as I pulled into my driveway. Though I did not understand their language,

intuitively I felt they were saying, 'now this is more like it.'

Inside. I escorted them up the carpeted stairway and showed them two, complete, tiled bathrooms adjacent to one another. I showed them the location of the towels and several bars of soap.

I could see their eyes widen with approval as I told them they could bathe anytime.

The Cubans seemed more relaxed as I showed them to the kitchen.

The sight of some dishes in the sink stirred up such a cleaning fervor in the two women that they instantly rolled up their sleeves, grabbed the biggest pots and used them for basins to wash the dishes.

In not more than five minutes, the dishes were all washed and the floor swept.

Amelia would have enjoyed that well disciplined performance, except the soap concentrate used would ordinarily last a full week.

In the living room Maria removed a long, red boot that reached practically up to her knee and held out her foot. It looked like a normal, healthy foot; no calluses, abrasions or defects of any kind.

As I turned to Geronimo to inform him that I was not a medical doctor, I saw in the palm of his hand a bill, ten dollars.

Maria wanted to return to the bedroom in the rear of the cafe to rest.

Three of my five sons, who were inadvertently becoming involved in the Cuban affair, were aware of my plight and began a search for Spanish dictionaries while I wanted to retreat.

Since the motorcycle was handy, I fled, leaving town on the old west road. A half hour later I returned from the north.

I went uptown to see Ted, the local grocer, wondering if he was willing to allow the Cubans to live in his spare apartment in exchange for clean up work in the store, as we had once discussed. But I would never find out on this particular visit, being drawn by Ted's voice in the rear yelling^ "the pizza is frozen."

I turned the corner and found Maria and Juana with Ted, who always thought he could improve communication with an increase in volume.

"They must be pretty smart to know what a pizza is," Ted remarked.

He quickly turned the two women over to my custody and urged me to see what food they wanted.

They must have read Ted's mind because Maria was already halfway down the aisle, holding a pound of chocolate chips. Juana saw how easy it was and grabbed a bag for herself. Beginning to think it was a lot of fun, she turned completely around to the opposite shelf and snatched a bag of orange candy.

Then both scurried to the grocery store entrance and, barefooted, they hightailed across the street with their loot to the cafe they despised.

Later. I brought some pizzas up for them from home. I knocked on the window of the front door, but nobody answered. After the third hard knock I assumed all were asleep.

At least they had something to eat, I thought, as I noticed the wrapper from the orange candies laying on top of a table, torn and empty.

I returned home with the undelivered pizzas.

Almost an hour later my son. Salty, who was almost fifteen, brought me the news that the Cuban women had been over to see the priest at the Catholic Church.

Unable to speak any Spanish it would have been very easy for Father Haskill to infer that these strange people in town were looking for a handout.

I was correct in my assumption. Already Father Haskill had made a call, soliciting some charitable Help from a lady parishioner.

I hurried up town just in time to witness the familiar woman, a pillar in the church, with a large paper bag in hand, marching past the café.

But she did not get past Juana, who was on the lookout for her.

In an instant. Juana's hands plunged into the lady's bag, ferreting about, as the charitable parishioner stood mesmerized by the sight of such uncouth conduct.

After pulling out two pairs of matching, white shoes Juana pulled the bag along, with the lady holding on to it, over to where her daughter, Maria, was standing. Now both women started to rummage through it as if they were at a remarkably cheap sale.

At last, Maria found a white pair of shoes which she liked and stepped into them with her bare feet while Juana flung an undesirable black pair into the bag and indelicately waved the lady off with the palm of her hand.

"Are they Chinese? I surely wouldn't want them at my house . . . and look at that . . ."

The lady just noticed that Juana had thrown away half of a sandwich.

"They don't seem to be very hungry," said the lady sarcastically, pointing to the ground.

Then. Juana, who claimed to be a college graduate, bent over, picked up the bread out of the dirt and finished eating it.

At last Peter had arrived. I had many things to know of my visitors and many questions to ask

"Why did they come to America?"

"To make money and to own a home."

"Did they know many Americans were out of work who would resent their being here?"

They knew, but they would persevere.

I told them they would not be permitted to beg from anyone because I wanted a greater dignity for them. If they needed something, they were to come to me.

"What did they need?"

Geronimo needed a pair of tennis shoes, a pair of shorts and a T shirt and Maria wanted a maternity outfit and a pair of tongs, Juana wanted a better place to live, with a family.

During our three way interview Juana was making numerous gestures, as if she had- a million pains.

Geronimo spoke of firing squads in existence in Havana.

Only the Russians and Cuban Communists were taking the supplies. Unless a person became a Communist, he was doomed to receive little or nothing.

Every six months he was alotted a pair of pants and a shirt.

He described how his left arm was yanked from its socket when he was seven. Now he cannot lift his left hand over his forehead.

Above all, the Cubans wanted to work. Their drive for work was insatiable, "for pay or no pay."

What a contrast in attitude with my teenage youngsters, I thought. Perhaps the Cubans had a lesson to teach them.

Was it possible now that I could actually tell somebody to do something around the house and it would be done . . . promptly.'

Within minutes after Peter departed we were loading up mattresses, bed frames, a chest of drawers and the only visible possessions of the Cubans', one suitcase and one full, paper bag.

I decided the basement would be sufficiently large and comfortably cool for them. We placed the double bed in a nook near the furnace for the sake of privacy. The single bed for the mother was placed arbitrarily around the corner, near a window.

Gradually Maria was beginning to reach out toward me by tapping me on the shoulder. Then, as if rowing a boat, she motioned with her arms for me to follow her. We went upstairs to a bathroom where she uncovered the shower.

After showing her how to turn it on, she nodded head approvingly and smiled briefly. For me that very first smile was a welcome contact.

Then Maria opened the medicine cabinet and methodically examined its medicinal contents.

All three had bathed, then doused themselves with a generous amount of talcum powder. This should have been a sedating experience for each . . . but it didn't last for very long.

Juana, always bolder in her demands, wanted to phone Miami.

I called Peter again for some extra interpretations. Fortunately, he was in.

Juana spoke to Peter about 30 seconds, then hung up. Since I had no idea what she said to him, I called Peter back.

"She wants me to come out immediately."

I informed Peter that we had made the move; they were settled in the cool basement and had just taken a shower.

"Well, what more do they want?" he asked with puzzlement.

It was Maria's turn next. She came with a piece of paper, torn from an ordinary grocery bag, with her brother's name printed on it. He was still at Fort Chaffee and she was concerned for his life because of the knifings which occurred there. She wanted me to get him out.

Geronimo wanted writing paper and an envelope so he could write to his 71 year old mother in Cuba.

Perhaps it was a good sign, I thought. The Cubans were establishing a home base and were now thinking of other concerns.

Yet I constantly wished I could speak with them directly.

Being July 5th, the shells of the fireworks the family expended the previous night were strewn about the lawn to the east of our huge brick dwelling.

I started to pick up the leftovers and Geronimo quickly joined me. I noticed his lit Harvester in his hand, which was an expensive habit for a poor man, and decided to borrow it to light a live firecracker.

Geronimo pulled back, fright etched on his face, as the explosive sound echoed in his ears.

Salty pieced together some Spanish words and, speaking with Maria, determined that the Cubans were afraid of the Fourth of July noises because they reminded them of gunfire.

During the first day in my home I discovered that Juana didn't know how to flush the toilet and Geronimo could not use a can opener. Maria was scooping the debris from the automatic sink disposal while I shoved it back in and pushed the button to make it go away.

Maria reminded me that there was no air conditioning as she began blowing down the front of her dress.

Before going to bed she removed a bottle of Excedrin from the medicine cabinet. She pointed to her head and used Geronimos name. He had a headache.

With our huge, brick house and broad expanse of land, trees and shrubs, it was not uncommon for our family to refer to our property as "the plantation."

The image of a black man working on it should confirm that, but it surely would not be expected to be typical for South Dakota. In spite of what it would appear like, Geronimo was anxious to work and the plantation was a good place for him to begin.

Sunday, July 6 No matter how religious or how Catholic the Cubans fancied themselves to be, they were not prepared to go to church as yet, not at St. Joseph's.

There were too many imperfections present for that sublime move. They would walk together, but probably all over the street. They would enter the church as if they were landlords . . . and their clothing supply was meager and colorless, causing them to stand out on a lower level compared with the regular churchgoers.

Yet the Cubans needed to attend church. It was their strong alternative to Communism in Cuba.

Geronimo's brass cross strung around his neck and a black bible, which he carried possessively in a bag, seemed to be a strong testimony of how the Cubans felt about their faith.

Amelia decided to drive them to another church in a much larger town where nobody was likely to turn a head or even care about the Cubans' presence.

Like little children going to a Sunday picnic they waved at me as they drove off.

After church they would go on a shopping spree.

I suggested that the ladies have their hair fixed. Also, Maria should have nail polish and her pierced ears should have earrings. If only she could allow her nails to grow; if only she could smile spontaneously instead of displaying that interminable poker face. Then, 1 thought, she could even radiate a feminine glow.

This was but the second day but, already, to look about the house is to see an infusion of a different mind.

These were "No" people. They were saying an emphatic "NO" to communism and continued to say "no" to other aspects of traditionalism which we. as a family, found comfortable. They would not hesitate to say "no" to me as an ultimatum even before feeling a personal comfort with me. Yet to me a "no" may have seemed too strong coming from these reactionaries, but to them it was a routine matter.

Allowing them to defy the structure and style of my living was part of making them feel comfortable here. I could accept it easily if my handkerchiefs were but folded differently, if the kitchen was always clean and the bathrooms scrubbed, but discovering bananas and canned goods in the freezer was indelicate. . . and the empty cans, which usually landed in the garbage pail, were somehow being stockpiled under the sink.

Maria would not allow herself to open the door of the refrigerator the first day. She would ask me for ice but would not take it directly.

The second day she turned completely self-sufficient. Now there was never any ice in the refrigerator; it could not manufacture it fast enough for her.

When Amelia and the refugees returned from the big town we had an elaborate meal together. Rice was a big food item for them.

The potentially wild, panic stricken Juana of yesterday was my target. If only she were content, then the others would follow suit.

Quietly we ate together. Juana had consumed a big helping of rice mixed with beans which assured me that she was becoming domesticated.

"Permisso," Geronimo uttered after eating. He looked at me for my reaction. I nodded my head, then he left the table.

I noticed that Juana's and Maria's hair was not done.

"There was nobody there experienced to do kinky hair," Amelia explained.

At the beauty shop Juana did not let the opportunity pass without using a sympathy technique. In fast-spoken Spanish she pleaded that Maria's hair be done, if not her own.

"We have come twenty miles and my daughter is pregnant."

Then she wiped her tearless eyes for effect.

Amelia thought they could have their hair done the following day when the manager was available.

Geronimo wanted to work and I would let him. We went to the orchard area, just north of the house.

If I could only tell him what to do exactly, I thought, as I looked about for work for the black man. I soon discovered that if I could point and say "si" or "no" I was in business.

I pointed at the weeds and said "si" and to the grapevine, "no." With a saw in hand Geronimo began tearing away the weeds and cutting small elms which were sprouting everywhere beneath the concord vines.

Amazingly, Carlton, 17, and Salty, both my sons, came and extolled the virtues of one like quiet and dutiful Geronimo. But unexpectedly they did more. They began helping him do the work.

It was short of a miracle because ordinarily a simple request that they do the same chore on their own would result in a dozen excuses. The 100 degree heat would be about the most cogent reason for their refusal to obey.

I asked my boys if Geronimo didn't really look like a slave working on my plantation.

"Quiet," they cautioned me together, "he'll hear you."

"He does what I ask, isn't that nice?"

Both sons sneered at the thought as they bent over in the powerfully hot sun.

"These people have respect for their elders. Before Geronimo left the dinner table today he asked me personally for my permission. Isn't that nice?" I taunted the unimpressed teen-ers.

Monday, July 7   Amelia and I would be working all day.
About noon Salty called.

"These people are all hyper. They're all dressed up waiting to get their hair done."

Amelia returned the call and told them it would be impossible to keep the hair appointment since there was no transportation available.

Being advised of the likelihood of cafeteria work near the close of the summer months. I acquired an application form for Geronimo for employment at the hospital, I then contacted Mark Spitzer at the Social Service Agency and inquired about a Social Security number for the Cubans. He would arrange an interview. "But they don't speak English."

Mark estimated it would take a week to find a Spanish interpreter.

At 5:30 we arrived home.

Something was wrong. There was a lackadaisical air about.

When I noticed the un-wiped breakfast crumbs on the kitchen table and the clearly uneven tablecloth, my fears were confirmed.

Maria emerged from the basement, devoid of any friendly greeting, and whispered to Amelia, "Geronimo has been crying because he has no paying work."

I simply did not know how to feel except pressured and, at the same time, helpless by this news.

At the large east window I stood pensively, noticing that my lengthy rows of hedges were trimmed nicely. But "Geronimo wanted paying work tomorrow"

, . . that was the intestinally painful message being repeated by Geronimo's wife as I stood immobilized by her pressing demands.

For the Cubans I could tell it was becoming a matter of either cleaning too hard and too much or else being negligent. They appeared to have a convincing way of telling me to do the cleaning myself if I did not suitably meet their ultimatum.

Amelia visited Geronimo downstairs, intending to verify Maria's story. He was looking at a magazine.

She uncovered no evidence whatsoever that he had been sad or looked tearful.

Later Maria informed us that Geronimo was not eating because he was sad. On interviewing him directly we discovered that he was truly not eating but not because he was sad. He was too fat.

Amelia interpreted Maria's guilt production for me as a common mechanism in the Spanish tradition. It was also a favorite technique of Filipinos.

Obviously a crying person or a sad person was intended to stir up in you feelings of sympathy . . . but having to prevaricate, to say what was not true, that was deceitful.

As I sat, drinking a can of warm pop because there was no ice left, Maria sat down next to me. She gently nudged me, wishing me to turn and look at her. I did. She pretended to be smoking. I turned away to have another swallow of pop and received another nudge. Then the smoking gestures came, one after another. It was clear to me that she had run out of cigarettes.

I coughed twice, demonstrating to Maria that cigarette smoking was harmful. She wasn't convinced, making it clear that Juana was the one who coughed, not she.

My 16 year old daughter, Crystal, thought the Cubans were "stinking up the place" and urged me not to buy the cigarettes.

As Maria persisted with her smoking gesticulations, it was apparent that the absence of nicotine was making her nervous. Finally, I relented, feeling most peculiar in doing what I truly never did before, buy a package of cigarettes.

In addition to the cigarettes for Maria I bought a few packs of cigars for Geronimo. When I handed him the cigars I verified Amelia's impression to my fullest satisfaction. Geronimo was neither tearful nor sad as he responded with a kind "gracias" and a wisp of a smile in exchange for the gift.

Now that I had removed the stumbling block, the caged mood of the Cubans, characterized by their strong desire to smoke and the inability to pay for it themselves, I expected that now at least one of them would be favorably disposed to attend to the kitchen table.

Geronimo and I motored to Spencer, a nearby community, ten miles west.

We played word games on the way. I pointed to an object and gave the proper English name. Geronimo would repeat the English word and the same word in Spanish.

If anything. I was sure he would remember "cow" forever.

Geronimo was unaware that my intention was to see a baseball game in Spencer.

When we arrived at the ball park the game was under way. As we watched the plays I became impressed with Geronimo's familiarity with baseball. He knew the English words for foul ball, strike and out and could identify the pitcher and catcher.

Then, with a surge of excitement, he pointed at the left fielder. It was Salty.

I decided that my duties as a parent were vital. Thus, I was not present at the ball game to serve the ends of exposing Geronimo to baseball primarily, but to watch Salty play, which I would have done under any circumstances.

After returning from Spencer I endeavored to share with Amelia some of the efforts I had made today for the betterment of the Cubans. I mentioned that I had acquired an employment application for the hospital and had contacted Social Security. . .but it was becoming increasingly impossible for me to squeeze in another word.

"Amelia, Amelia, Amelia," so crippled our casual conversation that I became suddenly mute with futility.

It was more "Amelia, Amelia, Amelia," as each of the two Cuban women vied for recognition, demanding that all three be employed by tomorrow.

Since we could not give prompt satisfaction to the urgent request of the Cuban women, Juana thought of one possible answer, to call Peter.

She called but was unsuccessful in reaching him.

The dimming of this last ray of hope frantically drove the two women from the table. Quickly they descended the basement stairs to plan further strategy.

After watching my son, Vernon, age 13. pitch in the park near our home this evening. Amelia and I invited Geronimo and Maria for a conference.

For an hour, with a dictionary in hand and Amelia at my side, we proceeded to explain to the couple about the importance of a Social Security number prior to employment in this country. I lifted my card from my wallet, displayed it and read off the numbers.

Furthermore, I informed them they would be signing up for food stamps tomorrow. I specifically emphasized that they would not be signing for a job, only for food stamps, "to buy things."

I had the distinct impression that there were no other relatives in Cuba except Geronimo's mother until I noticed a letter being sent by Juana to an Alberto De La Cruz.

Amelia questioned the Cubans and uncovered that Maria had four brothers.

Later on, Juana approached me, waving her arms over her head. Her signals were different from Maria's but they meant the same: "follow me." Like a robot I walked behind the fast stepping old lady up the thirteen steps to the second-floor bathrooms.

In spite of the fact that she had already showered three times she continued to need somebody to turn on the faucet.

The Cubans retired. All was quiet as Amelia and I sat contentedly at the kitchen table, exploring some next moves.

Who could speak Spanish? Who did we know who knew somebody who could speak it? we asked ourselves.

There was a professor in Iowa who volunteered to teach Cuban refugees English. Amelia had read about it in the Sioux City newspaper a month ago.

Also. Amelia could recall, the name of a Mrs. Carreras. Who had taught English in Havana for five years. Because she was an elderly woman Amelia could not be certain of her accessibility.

I made my decision to postpone the two week vacation I planned to Pennsylvania. I could not conceivably leave Amelia alone to cope with the foibles and idiosyncrasies of the refugees singlehandedly. .

Earlier this evening I had paid a visit to Father Haskill.

I was compelled to inform him about the newcomers in the town. Besides, since he had his finger on the pulse of the town I was curious to know what reactions were occurring.

Father Haskill indeed confirmed that Maria and Juana came to his door looking destitute and barefooted. Charitably he gave them $15 and invited a parishioner to provide them with shoes. He was not aware of any bad town publicity.

"After the shoe incident the family vanished from sight," he said curiously.

"That's because I sheltered them in my home to keep them from wandering about."

Father offered to order Spanish missalettes and would greet them with a special kindness when they appeared in church for daily mass.

He was especially interested in knowing what enlightenment he could provide to his parishioners when asked.

"Tell others they arc victims of religious persecution. Tell them they are impoverished and own nothing but the clothing on their backs. Tell them that they preferred Christianity to Communism," I suggested.

Tuesday, July 8 I promised myself to make four calls today, to the Cuban teacher, to Mark Spitzer at Social Security, to Lucille Millner of the County Social Welfare and Sister Nadine of the Catholic Social Services in Sioux Falls.

My effort in contacting Mrs. Carreras was fruitful.

She graciously offered to spend the day with the Cubans and accompany them to the Social Security Office.

I called Mark immediately. He was pleased to have Mrs. Carreras serve as interpreter for his agency.

He inquired of the Cuban family's status.

"Asylum status."

Under the circumstances the mother, who was 69, could be eligible for SSI benefits.

It would take about 10 days after application for the Social Security cards to arrive, Mark estimated.

Catholic Social Services, who served as an intermediary in acquiring my refugees, did not know of their arrival.

"What are they like?" queried Sister Nadine.

"They eat pizzas, drink coke, and smoke like a wet fire. My icemaker cannot keep up with their demands."

"New benefits were approved for the Cubans. They're eligible for medicaid."

"If that means maternity care and delivery benefits, I'm all for it."

It did. Also, like the Vietnamese, they were eligible to receive financial assistance.

"Send me the papers immediately," I requested thankfully.

Carlton would drive the refugees to the Court House in Spencer today for their one o'clock appointment with Lucille Millner.

"They can't receive food stamps if they're living with you," Miss Millner said on the phone when I informed her of Carlton's intention to bring the Cuban's for the stamps.

When I promised to provide the Cubans with a private refrigerator for their food, Lucille conceded to issue the stamps.

To my delight she even had second thoughts about the second refrigerator. It was not necessary if some demarcation could be improvised between my food and their food in the same refrigerator.

She didn't think that they would be in violation of any rules if they ate ten of my pizzas to every one of theirs I wiped out.

Geronimo greeted me with a "trabajo" greeting and a casual smile, which he had been manifesting a bit more frequently recently, as he left through the rear entrance to water the vegetable garden.

Intending to broaden my Spanish vocabulary I reached for the dictionary, which was assuming the status of the Bible in our home. I opened it.

Trabajo, trabajo . . . work. Damn," I exclaimed, "it meant work." Geronimo thought the food stamp interview was a job interview.

That's why he was smiling, he thought he had a job.

Maria darted up the stairs yelling, "Amelia, Amelia, Amelia," just as the sound of our footsteps reached her ears.

"Amelia Amelia," she shrieked at me.

I wasn't Amelia but she wanted me to bring her to Amelia. No, I wouldn't create that kind of delivery system. Besides, Amelia was changing her clothes.

Maria split, screeching even louder, searching all seventeen rooms for the elusive Amelia.

The temperature was a hundred.

When I turned to the ice container in the refrigerator, the story was the same: no ice.

When Amelia arrived in the kitchen, followed by a shadow called Maria and her incessant prattling, she advised the girl to drink milk instead of coke. Alert Juana, who was faster than the blinking of an eye and ever so faithful to her duty as a mother, overheard Amelia's prescription and promptly fetched a gallon of milk and set it on the table before Maria. Then we beheld a miracle. Maria drank her first glass of milk.

Amelia, pointing to Crystal who was a tall five foot seven, said "that's from drinking milk."

We all drove to watch Salty play his second baseball game without Amelia. She was attending a meeting at a farmhouse near Spencer.

During the game Juana was as active as a cow's tail near a manure pile on a dreadfully hot day. She absolutely could not remain unmoving. Not knowing where to look she fitfully looked everywhere, at least once.

As I sat next to her on a bench, behind the catcher, her elbow poked my ribs repeatedly. Then she would point at my wristwatch and cradle her head in her hands as if it were nap time.

The game was over.

I realized it was not the easiest game to follow, not with restless Juana at my side.

It was impossible for the fans to overlook the spectators from Cuba, especially Geronimo and his midnight blackness.

As we walked toward our wagon, we moved with a small crowd.

Juana made herself obvious by interacting with a small child who was being carried by her mother, throwing kisses to her.

"Awe, she really likes children, doesn't she," the mother said purringly.

We drove to the nearby farm house where Amelia was attending an Arts Festival Committee meeting.

Soon we were being escorted to a living room congested with about seven people and assorted papers which cluttered the floor. It was in that very room that Amelia and I discovered the treasure, Anna Stein. She was born in Peru and could speak superb Spanish.

Our presence prompted the immediate closure of the meeting as we prepared ourselves for fellowship in the presence of a Spanish interpreter.

Immediately we knew what was on Juana's mind.

"I want work tomorrow. I want a room alone, right away."

Geronimo, calm and deliberate, measuring his words carefully and the complete opposite of Juana in every way, told her politely that she could wait a couple of months more because, after all, she waited 21 years under Castro to leave Cuba.

Maria sat solemnly, passively, almost as if frightened.

Could she be experiencing a cigarette withdrawal? I wondered. At least I was positive that she had not smoked in at least five hours.

Shortly Anna, with her linguistic skill, pulled Geronimo right out of his casual demeanor. He was actually speaking briskly and his hands were moving about as if he were conducting an orchestra.

Only then did I learn that Geronimo worked in a Textile Mill until the fibers affected his health and that Vincente De La Cruz Sanchez was the brother of Maria who remained at Fort Chaffee.

Anna promised to talk to Edward, her husband, to sponsor Vincente.

The Cubans appeared delighted with the prospect ot having Vincente with them. Even pained Maria managed a sign of joy as her thick lips parted in a smile while Geronimo clapped his hands. Only volatile Juana, Vincente's mother, was containing her exuberance for some unbeknown reason by merely shifting the position of her legs.

1 cautioned Anna to pursue the matter of sponsorship more carefully.

"Why didn't Vincente arrive with the others?" I asked. "Could the authorities know more than the Cubans were telling? Could he be a criminal?"

Anna promptly asked the Cubans if Vincente was a law breaker.

"No, no, no . . ."

Geronimo thought the question was too incredible.

"But why didn't Vincente come with you &o South Dakota?"

"They told us they had only three tickets," Maria said, finally speaking out.

"What kind of tickets?"

"For the plane, to fly to South Dakota."

Three tickets, not four?. . ."but if you were together?"

"We were not together. Vincente was in another camp, Barracca 1060. We saw him once," Geronimo explained.

"But why didn't they bring you together?"

"They didn't."

"Why?"

"Because he came alone on another boat, one month earlier."

"So. he had been there one month longer and he had not left yet?"

"Because Maria is pregnant we came out first. They sent out the families first."

"At Fort Chaffee they stab you for a cigarette." Said Geronimo.

Maria's face turned an instant crimson.

I explained to the refugees that I preferred no publicity for the moment. First they should know the community better, be employed and independently settled. Then their epic in America could be called a success story.

Geronimo expressed his deep appreciation for the loving care he and his family received in my home.

I told him he was my son.

"And your children are my brothers," he said warmly, and told of the profound love he felt from the hearts of the American people.

The flood of appreciation was deeply touching.

"Why don't we get Vincente?" I whispered to Amelia.

Geronimo received high grades for poise and charm.

He spoke remarkably well for a tenth grader. He spoke in eloquent, feeling terms as he expressed the honor he was experiencing to have been invited to that humble farm house. Then we all rose to leave.

Geronimo's enchanting manner was so moving, it served as ample stimulus for the Arts Festival Committee to think of originating a Spanish Club. It also gave Anna a personal satisfaction, to invite the Cubans to dinner on Saturday.

It was past 10:30 when we arrived home. Salty, naked to the waist just finished heating a dish of noodles and meat sauce. He felt Juana tap him on the shoulder just as he was about to indulge himself.

"No, Geronimo."

Without another word, Juana scooped up the plate, which Salty prepared for himself, and fled to the basement.

Salty was piqued. He stood up, indignantly beating his bare chest.

"What the hell is going on here?"

"Inconsiderate, isn't she."

"You're a stupid one for bringing them here."

"But we can handle it," I said quietly, as Salty's muscles tensed for a fight.

"Mother," I called, "we got a hungry boy here: fix him some good food . . . now."

Carlton invited me upstairs to his bedroom.

"I didn't show them anything, dad. This is what I got."

In the envelope Carlton handed me was $160 worth of food coupons.

". . . and they will get the same for each of the next two months. After the third month you re-register them."

Wednesday, July 9 Amelia and I were up early. We wanted to be certain the refugees were awake and ready to accompany us.

We were going to meet Mrs. Carreras. the teacher who actually lived in Cuba twenty years ago.

We arrived in time to see a 60 year old, wiry lady already waiting for us in a white Ford in the south parking lot of the hospital. She was generously contributing a whole afternoon for the Cuban cause. She would accompany them and interpret for them at the Social Security Office, visit the Medical Clinic for Maria's checkup and assist them in grocery shopping. Her motive? ... An obligation to repay the Cubans for years of kindness she received as a guest in their country.

They are a very generous and sharing people," she discovered.

Holding a white envelope, I told Mrs. Carreras we had food stamps and encouraged her to buy a small amount of food initially until the Cubans learned the American style of shopping.

This morning I called Sister Nadine and asked her to locate Maria's brother, Vincente De La Cruz, Area 4, Barracca 1060, Fort Chaffee, Arkansas. I would sponsor him.

Later this afternoon Amelia and I arrived at the home of Mrs. Carreras, our pre arranged rendezvous, where the three Cubans would be awaiting us.

The temperature was a scorching 104 degrees and most of the food purchased by the Cubans was perishable, $80 worth. We quickly transferred the food from the hot trunk of Mrs. Carreras' Ford to the blue wagon and drove off immediately, waving our thanks to Mrs. Carreras and promising to call her.

We arrived home a half hour later.

The Cubans quickly unloaded the groceries but surprisingly carried all the food possessively to their quarters in the basement. The groceries were lined up on the stairs, one sack per step.

Then Juana came upstairs in a state of agitation.

She was hugging and kissing everything in sight. Accompanying the hugs and kisses for Amelia and myself was a word, "solo."

I honestly believed Juana was being effusive in her gratitude for the day's achievements. But no, her appreciation was being offered for a future happening, for something about to happen.

Geronimo was removing the bed sheets from the double bed and began lifting the mattress. The day's work and the high temperature had been fatiguing enough but this rearrangement was a totally unanticipated about face.

Geronimo and Maria were returning to the cafe.

Perhaps it was advantageous for Geronimo and Maria to be removed from Juana and her harassment. Juana could have a place of "her own" and the married couple could enjoy their privacy. Of course Maria, being pregnant, would be relieved of the burden of walking up stairs: these were my thoughts as Geronimo and I struggled with the double bed mattress, trying to maneuver it up the stairs without knocking over the bags of food.

Finally we were loaded, a box spring with a double mattress, frames, sheets and pillow cases; a chest of drawers and, of course, one small suitcase and $80 worth of groceries.

After this cyclonic move there could only be a peaceful aftermath, I surmised, as I sped off on my bicycle to the post office,

They bad made their decision and it was a closed book. They wouldn't starve and had all necessary conveniences to endure under a roof.

I was very confident they could handle it.

Because of the heat my night was practically sleepless.

I required an hour's nap before counseling my clients at my uptown Marriage and Family Counseling Center.

At eight o'clock I was up and dressed, pedaling toward town. I noticed Amelia strolling with Maria and Juana on either side of her. A serious exchange was going on as I cycled past.

Later I would learn that Maria had left Geronimo at the cafe and wandered down the street weeping, that Juana was crying also because the family group was split.

"I worked so hard for her to be raised, now she is leaving me for a man," Juana protested pitifully.

Crystal suggested a therapy for Juana to cope with her distress, a warm shower and a nap.

To understand the meaning of the quick turn of events I called Mrs. Carreras.

"All day they were snapping at each other. At every opportunity Juana would whisper to me, I don't like that man. "

Juana would tell the couple, "I don't want to live with you and pray to God you leave me alone."

In a restaurant, where they came for a drink, Juana said of Maria, "Isn't she a beautiful daughter?" and of herself, "but I am old."

At her home Mrs. Carreras offered Maria "milk or lemonade." Juana decided it would be milk.

Geronimo would not tolerate Juana's interference and, practically bursting a vessel, blurted a lusty, "No, lemonade." Maria had lemonade.

It was 9:30. Though their possessions were at the cafe, what of the whereabouts of Geronimo and Maria? They were together, downstairs.

Though Juana was in their midst, I invited only the married couple upstairs for a conference, specifically directing Juana to be absent.

As we seated ourselves Carlton phoned from the upstairs extension.

"The old lady is creeping up the stairs."

I quickly confirmed Carlton's message and motioned Juana back.. Then I shut the basement door.

We told the couple of our great respect for them and realized that Juana was overbearing at times.

Maria gave a surprised look, protectively denying any difficulties with Juana.

Geronimo expressed concern for the eavesdropping member of the family. He wanted her to have medication. For about eight years she was "a very unreasonable lady," admitted Geronimo, following the desertion by her husband.

Amelia chanced the bold interpretation that Juana was too demanding and treated Maria like a child. Maria squirmed but did not refuse the meaning of Amelia's words.

Geronimo apologized for moving back and forth but found it imperative to escape Juana or else they would suffer a nervous breakdown.

We told the couple of the call to have Vincente come to be with them. The news brightened them up immediately but Maria was unreasonably impatient. She wanted him here tomorrow.

I asked Carlton to bring a radio in from the garage, the small, black, portable one, thinking that some added entertainment might relieve the loneliness they could be feeling and, besides, they could tune in something else besides Juana.

When I handed Geronimo the radio, he smiled and gave me a double "gracias." I showed him how to use the radio and hooked up the antenna for him. He then turned the knob to a musical program, sat down in one of the two chairs near his bed, and relaxed.

About eleven this evening Maria and Geronimo decided to procure their sandwich meat from the cafe, but they wanted an escort. I decided to accompany them.

We walked together about 100 yards. I stopped, but the couple kept walking until they noticed they were alone. Geronimo stood undaunted by my absence but Maria began to run toward me in a frenzy. I waved her on.

"Go, go. It's alright."

With further insistence she stopped, turned and cautiously walked toward Geronimo. She grabbed his arm tightly and both walked together in the darkness.

In about 20 minutes the fearful wanderers arrived. They carried with them about half of their food supply, mostly the meats, and six large bottles of coke.

I placed the meats in the freezer since room in the refrigerator was practically non-existent. Maria had been putting her cookies and peanuts in there to cool off. Now she was shoving a large bottle of coke in the freezer for overnight.

How were Geronimo and Maria sleeping tonight? I had absolutely no idea. I only knew their double bed was in one place and they in another.

Amelia suggested that we put our guests to work tomorrow, washing the windows.

I would call Mrs. Carreras about the suggestion she made earlier. She had a friend with an extra room. It Juana wanted to go "solo," this could be her grand opportunity. With $238 SSI, she could probably live there comfortably for $75 a month. But the SSI would take two or three weeks, Mark Spitzer said. She would have to wait that long.

As for Geronimo, he could be eligible to work through SETA, a government subsidized work program, but he would first require a Social Security number. If he proved himself in a two month period under SETA, then he could be eligible for regular employment.

Thursday, July 10   The temperature is 103.

I called Carlton and suggested that he keep the Cubans occupied.

"They put oil on everything. They eat bananas and put oil on them. They're greasy people, dad."

The married couple are alright but the grandma is hounding me. What can I do?'"

"Put her to work cleaning the windows."

Mrs. Carreras, called.

With an I 94 designation, she discovered the Cubans were eligible to work immediately and did not require a work permit. Her news was fantastic, I told her, but we had one overriding deficiency, work.

Mrs. Carreras' friend, the one with the extra room, was receptive to having Juana live there if she would assist in caring for two dogs and a canary.

I invited Mrs. Carreras to my home, recommending that we try family counseling with the Cubans. She was very willing to come, tomorrow at eight, and would bring a friend who had taught Spanish at the University.

The Spanish linguists seemed to be gladly emerging out of the woodwork, alleviating our own sense of separation from the Cubans.

I glanced at my calendar. Two days had passed and there was no call from Sister Nadine concerning Vincente.

When Amelia and I entered our house following' a day at work, the domestic scene was unbelievably tranquil. The Cubans were not harassing us at the door with trivial questions. A loud signal from the first female Cuban to spot us, alerting the other to swarm about us, never occurred.

The house was pleasantly in order and supper was prepared. We sat down at the table. Maria sat with us, watching our faces to see what degree of satisfaction her reddish looking rice mixed with slices of hot dog and lettuce, swimming in vinegar, would bring to them.

Though I had hardly started to treat my taste buds I heard: "gusto?"

"Gusto," I replied, brightening Maria's life instantly as I joylessly ate the tasteless rice and swallowed a considerable amount of vinegar with the lettuce.

"Gusto?" she asked again, never batting an eyelash until I finished.

With a "mucho gusto" I made Maria's existence justified.

Then I descended to the cool, cool basement and smelled the heavy scent of cigar smoke.

Geronimo had done some renovating, I noticed. He devised a drape enclosure in the corner of the basement for privacy. But I could not see what he was harboring behind those thick layers of draping. Only later I learned that Geronimo and Salty had returned the bed we had, so suddenly, whisked off yesterday.

Salty informed me that the Cubans had popcorn and coke for lunch.

Opening the freezer, I removed some black bananas, frozen cucumbers, apples and lettuce, all ruined.

Crystal complained that the upstairs bathrooms were beginning to stink because "they are putting their poop paper in the waste basket."

Usually when Geronimo spotted me outside, he would come out also, thinking he could help me with some chore. This evening I acquired a wheelbarrow and some cement to do some plastering. Barefooted, he took over, handling the 100 pounds with ease, and completed the work.

This evening, the atmosphere was casual. Geronimo, who is left-handed, played catch with Vernon. On the porch, Amelia was teaching Maria and Juana how to play cards.

The setting was so naturally pleasant, I was tempted to let well enough alone and cancel our family counseling plan.

The temperature in the house was 90 degrees. I weakened to the pleas of Carlton and turned on the central air conditioning.

Salty, who took pride in the freshness of his room, was equally gratified but soon he experienced a disadvantage: His room was beginning to smell like Geronimo's cigar smoke.

Tomorrow Amelia would take the day off from work. She would teach Juana and Maria how to sew. She bought material and would make a dress for each of them.

I would take to the hospital Geronimo's application for work, which we completed in a remarkably flimsy manner.

Friday, July 11 I received the call from Sister Nadine which I awaited.

Contact was made with Fort Chaffee but they needed more information about Vincente De La Cruz. He should have a second name. There were three Vincente De La Cruz's at Fort Chaffee and one had already been sent off.

I checked the name again and did, indeed, discover a third name, "Sanchez." Sister Nadine would check out the new name.

Mrs. Carreras called. Maria phoned her to come at 5:30 and wondered if I knew of the time change. Since Amelia was at home, that made it alright, I explained. We would expect her and her guest at 5:30.

Again the domestic scene was pleasant when I arrived home. Juana immediately escorted me to the dining room table. She wanted to show me how nicely she prepared the table to accommodate eight.

The house was exceptionally clean and orderly, no doubt the product of Amelia's presence.

I had an engagement at the Counseling Center this evening.

Before departing Maria accosted me with a plate of rice and a pork chop smelling of garlic. Then she detained me until I paid her off in "gustos."

Just as Mrs. Carreras and Mr. Jensen, her attorney friend, had arrived I was leaving for my office.

In one hour I returned and found Amelia, Mrs. Carreras, Mrs. Jensen, Geronimo, Juana and Maria chatting in the living room. As I sat down next to Juana I made my curiosity known about the two name system.

Mr. Jensen elucidated, "Normally the first last name is the father's last name; the second last name is the mother's last name.

In Vincente's case De La Cruz was the mother's name and the last name, Sanchez, was the uncle's name because he went to live with his uncle. The father's name was Guava.

Mr. Jensen asked Maria how Vincente was called.

"Either De La Cruz Sanchez or Sanchez De La Cruz."

Geronimo was quite certain it was De La Cruz Sanchez, the name I gave to Sister Nadine.

I asked Mrs. Cameras for an update.

"We learned that Juana is nervous and very worried. From one side of her mouth she is saying she will go 'solo'; from the other, her only daughter must take care of her.

As for Maria, for a half hour she proclaimed why she could not live with her mother. Yet, when asked why she brought her along, she replied, 'I'm her only daughter.' "

"If she is living alone," said Maria with concern, "that would be impossible to bear, because mamma would feel as if she had died."

"True," Juana agreed with a noble air, her nose pointing upward, "if I can't live with them I'm going to die."

"Then die,"`I echoed, "at least you won't all die."

"That's alright, I will live alone ... for a time."

"Forever," I said emphatically.

". . .and they can go by themselves."

Now that you've said it, Juana, mean it."

Juana laughed, being amused by the silly conversation.

Geronimo reminded us that, in Cuba, Juana was a frantic woman. "In one minute she could run all over Havana."

"Because my mother is nervous, I am nervous. She wants me to do things for her and not for him. I suffered a lot because of her."

"Well, Maria, you have a choice. You can continue to suffer or else you can grow up. Juana doesn't mind if you and Geronimo suffer on account of her; then why should you care if she suffers . . . But she is strong, she will survive."

"She won't let me be boss," Geronimo complained. "She contradicts me. She interferes and turns Maria's mind against my wishes. She promises to change many times, but does not keep her word.

"I would propose a new attitude for you: first, you should stop suffering on account of Juana and second, you should stick together as one."

Geronimo left the group followed by Maria.

Maria returned and Juana left, yelling Geronimo's name. There was a commotion in the basement, as if Juana were aggravating Geronimo.

The noises in the basement ceased.

Juana returned to her former seat, next to mine, crying. "When she cries, I cry," said Maria, "because she makes me nervous."

"Juana, when you are crying you are hurting your daughter, now stop it."

I advised Maria to tell Juana that Geronimo comes first and she was to do it while looking into her eyes.

She did so exactly.

Next I told her to tell Juana to stop hurting her with crying.

Maria did the job without hesitation.

Finally Geronimo returned complaining of a headache.

"Maybe I should have a headache too," Maria stated, laughingly.

Now that Geronimo was present, I wanted him to know the impactful words which Maria spoke to Juana so courageously, that he came first, that mamma should cease hurting them with her tears.

After Mrs. Carreras gave the appropriate information to Geronimo I asked the Cubans how they felt about the meeting.

Geronimo called it "very good," Maria referred to it as a "good idea" and Juana said she liked it. Then she concluded, "I'll live by myself."

Mrs. Carreras was curious to see the cafe because she could not fully understand why the Cubans rejected it. "My God," she exclaimed, "it's a roof over their heads."

We moved along together as one group but Juana stopped suddenly at the end of the walk and never moved, even when Maria called her to hurry.

We entered the cafe from the main street entrance.

I flicked on the first light switch and the low paneled ceiling came into view. With the help of a second set of lights the entire front portion of the cafe lit up exposing a refrigerator, a microwave, a pizza stove, a sink and several game machines.

"In Cuba this is a palace," proclaimed Mrs. Carreras.

Meanwhile, Juana stealthily entered the cafe from the rear entrance. She came into view for an instant, then disappeared like a phantom.

"Why did you leave this wonderful place?" Mrs. Carreras asked, turning to Maria who cowered next to Geronimo.

"I know," she said, "you were afraid because you didn't have your mamma with you."

Then, with an uncanny strangeness, Maria asked Amelia to be her number one mamma. Mrs. Carreras was requested to become Maria's second mamma.

"You're a married woman carrying a baby. What you need is to be a woman, not a child," said Mrs. Carreras disgustingly.

As we strolled homeward following our inspection tour Attorney Jensen said he was a general practitioner of law but did not enjoy divorce cases.

Saturday, July 12   Amelia thought that the worse should be over. Anna Stein called to say that she would be arriving early to deliver the Cubans to Crazy Days, a celebration and parade in Spencer.

Amelia was participating in wedding preparations at the local community hall and would be occupied all day.

Carlton was involved in painting some display signs for the approaching Arts Festival. Working in the kitchen, he was keenly sensitive to the fast-speaking Cubans in the basement.

"They're at it again," he would react intermittently.

Juana spent much of her time tidying up. There was never an unclean cup in the sink now.

Sitting in the living room reading, I was struck with the sound of the washing machine stopping prematurely. Investigating I discovered that Juana stopped the machine midway through the wash and was inserting another load of dirty clothes.

Juana's efforts to substitute quantity for quality were practically mischievous.

The daily routine for Juana was keeping busy. She was truly in her glory when someone would tell her what to do because then she could feel the greatest impact of approval. Alone she was aimless, chaotic, or repetative.

Sometimes she might be resting on the front porch, a blue rosary in hand, her mouth barely moving in prayer, gazing skyward. Her relationship with God was an open book, He was her friend.

Tomorrow she wanted to attend church. It was Sunday.

Juana's fondness for children had been demonstrated. Throwing kisses to them depicted her as both motherly and having concern for the innocent. At times, however, her ardor carried her far afield.

This morning, as I sat reading the newspaper, I heard "doaktor, doaktor." An unfamiliar child, barely 3 years old, was standing by my side. My first impulse was to tell Juana to put the girl back where she found her ... Then I did it myself.

Giving further thought to last night's counseling, I made a decision: Juana would not go with the couple to crazy days, it was time for a trial separation.

With help from the dictionary, I gave them my verdict:

"Geronimo and Maria goes with Anna, Juana, No."

Surprisingly, my announcement was received without a ripple of protest.

When-Anna and Edward Stein arrived at 1:30, Maria's appearance was enhanced by her yellow maternity outfit. Blotches of white talcum were visible on her neck.

As the couple entered Anna requested instructions.

"Geronimo might eat lightly because he wanted to diminish his paunch and Juana would not be going along for the sake of the couple's togetherness."

Anna and Edward wanted to buy the couple something.

I said, "Maybe a little. Probably they should not be conditioned to feel as if everything is free."

As the Stein's prepared to leave 1 remembered one, final reminder . . . "try not to tire them, it can make them irascible."

I backed off and stepped into Juana who stood behind me, suspensefully awaiting ignition. The car started, backing out slowly. I pulled at Juana's sleeve, intending to interrupt her trance-like state as the car sped out of sight. She lurched backwards and commenced praying her beads which she held in the palm of her hand.

The married couple were truly separated from Juana for the first time since they left Cuba by 10 miles of South Dakota farmland.

Later on in the afternoon, when Amelia returned home, Juana asked why she wasn't taken to Spencer with Anna.

"Because we want you with us."

"Why didn't you let her go," fired Salty, "Crazy Days would be the right place for her."

I had serious thoughts of having the Cubans come to Mass tomorrow, to St. Joseph's. With the numerous baths they were taking they were undoubtedly clean and, if cleanliness were next to Godliness, then they were certainly Godly.

Furthermore, their clothing was attractive and colorful. Their shoes were store-bought and they wore nothing begged or pilfered.

Tim, my oldest son, arrived for an evening's swim in the swimming pool across the street. It required about four minutes for Amelia to unlock the pool gate for Tim. In that time Juana had surreptitiously called Mrs. Carreras informing her of her loneliness. She expected to have her come immediately.

Amelia invited Juana to the park to see the children and gave her a ride on the swing.

Meanwhile, Juana asked frequently about Anna's return.

Amelia told Timothy that she noticed some reaction from the people with whom she worked at the Community Center. A farmer's wife inquired if the Cubans were receiving welfare and asked why the government wasn't taking care of the farmers in that way.

The ladies were quite curious why I made the move to sponsor the refugees. It gave Amelia an opportunity to divulge my philosophy on the matter:

"There are three things a person should do with his life, be good to his family, be good to his country, and be good to the world."

Amelia thought some of the prissy ladies of the town were frightfully unenlightened because none understood what it meant to live under oppression ... so Amelia told her story.

She described her experiences under the Japanese occupation of the Philippines and how her uncle had his teeth knocked out because he refused to bow to a Japanese sentry.

Finally, Anna and Edward returned after hosting the Cuban couple for nine and a half hours.

To Juana's complete delight, Anna promised her that next Sunday it would be her turn to be taken to Spencer for the day.

For the next half hour Maria and Geronimo soaked in the pool.

Before retiring, they told Amelia they would be sleeping late and would not be attending church.

Sunday, July 13 Juana, Amelia and I would venture forth boldly to St. Joseph's.

In her bright orange dress Juana's appearance was becoming to the occasion.

The church attendance, less than usual, was probably attributable to the wedding festivities last evening.

As we entered the church, a sense of uneasiness overcame me because bodily, she was there; she, who brought the used shoes at Father Haskill's request; she, who Maria and Juana treated so brazenly; she, who labeled them Chinese and would bar them from her home.

With the assistance of one deep breath, I moved forward. We began a threesome procession, Amelia first, Juana, then I. To the very front of the church we marched to the beat of turning heads.

Father Haskill spied us immediately from his elevated perch at the altar.

Throughout the service I had one eye on Juana. The cleaning out of the corners of her eyes with her fingers and running the palm of her hand over her face were immediately noticeable.

Occasionally her legs would bounce. She prayed but ultimately her prayers issued forth audibly as a contaminated mixture of two languages. For singing she substituted humming.

The gospel was timely. In fact, I was so amazed at its appropriateness, I began to believe that Father Haskill had improvised the subject matter of the gospel for this solitary occasion. But no, that was impossible since the gospel read was standard in all Catholic churches.

Could it have been a divine hand that brought us boldly, as a live illustration, to the front of the church with that one particular lady in attendance and then to hear recited, word for word, the story of the Good Samaritan?

I thought it appropriate for us to wait until the church was vacated before leaving.

As soon as I estimated the. correct moment, I rose and turned . . . and shuddered. The church was completely empty except for a solitary female, sitting alone at the very rear.

It was she, my nemesis, unstirred, sitting strategically in a spot where we would practically brush against her as we walked by.

In an act of clumsiness of my own making, I stumbled shamefully and practically fell bodily on top of the lady at the very instant of passing.

Outside of the church Juana received one kind "hello" and one wave from a car.

Though waving was very commonplace in our tiny town we, nevertheless, permitted Juana to believe what was extremely vital to her, that she was being singled out.

About one o'clock Geronimo approached me, requesting to do more cement work on the patio. Though I appreciated his offer, the work would need to be delayed. Presently I was scheduled to play softball with the South Dakota Tigers.

It was the fourth inning when I glanced at the bleachers. A black man was sitting there with the white people.

Geronimo was emerging from his compartment in my home in a civil, confident fashion.

At the 7th inning, Geronimo was gone. The couple had proceeded up town after Amelia had given Geronimo a dollar for pop.

Ted, the grocer, called later. He needed to reassure me that the Cuban couple were well behaved people. He had given them change for the dollar and was pleased to report that Geronimo placed the correct change in the pop machine.

"How wonderful . . . a minor breakthrough." I thought. They took an excursion uptown without being fearful and learned how to master a pop machine.

Geronimo was progressing rapidly in his orientation to American life while Maria's trepidation would not allow her to forsake her traditional ways.

This afternoon we were particularly pleased because Maria was genuinely attempting to speak a couple of English words.

A lighted cigarette in hand we heard her say, "no monkeys."

At first we had no inkling of what she meant. Then, by holding up her lighted cigarette, she gave us a clue. She was saying, "no smoking."

Amelia hastened to point out Maria's incongruity because, though she appeared to be espousing "no smoking," she was indeed smoking. Taking the message to heart. Maria promptly dropped the cigarette down the sink drain.

Besides adhering tenaciously to the use of her native tongue, Maria was also uninspired to experiment with new food. Literally, she would not touch a plum or a nectarine. Instead she requested the avocado and mango.

Amelia explained to her that these fruits were both rare and expensive in South Dakota.

Meanwhile, Juana was spending the day memorizing a one liner: "I go to the doaktor at 1:50 p.m. Friday with Mrs. Carreras for a general checkup."

The day's quietude was a pleasant experience.

As our rapport with the Cubans improved we decided to implement some regulations. First, smoking would be forbidden in the basement; second, since their taste buds favored such morsels as rice and garlic with bits of meat chopped up in a load of beans, Amelia requested that they cook enough only for themselves.

Anna called to report on the Saturday visit to Crazy Days. She thought Maria was exceptionally expressive in venting her feelings.

There was an unexpected gossip in the streets. The Cubans were being called by an unforgiving term, beggars. Anna, a gracious host, defended them, claiming the fault lay with some impoverished gypsies who were passing through.

After dining, the couple conversed about music, dancing and other kinds of entertainment. They were captivated by Anna's small house, estimating they could own such a $50,000 dwelling in three or four years if both of them worked hard. In their dream house they desired a T.V. and stereo.

When all this was achieved, then they would visit a friend in Miami.

Geronimo and Maria declined any gift from the Steins except a carton of cigarettes.

They purchased bakery rolls using their own food stamps.

During the visit Anna learned that Geronimo's left arm was wrenched loose from its socket when he was born.

Anna agreed to bring Geronimo to complete a job application at a nearby belt plant. Amelia had already made the appointment for him.

This evening I learned from Ted that he had been searching for clean-up help in his meat-cutting area and his wife, Pauline, would welcome assistance with her domestic chores.

When I recommended the Cubans for the job, Ted hesitated. He was pondering the impact of public opinion and how it could conceivably harm his business.

Monday, July 14   Mrs. Carreras called very early this morning. "Where is Juana?"

I immediately apologized for my ignorance because I had no knowledge of any mysterious arrangement between them.

I informed Mrs. Carreras of the projected plan which I deemed authentic, namely, on Friday Maria was scheduled for a checkup and Juana would have a physical. If other arrangements were being made then, I suggested, Juana was falsifying our intentions.

I apologized to Mrs. Carreras for the inconvenience and reminded her what an adventuresome busybody Juana can become with a phone number at her finger tips.

Mrs. Carreras was kind to call Friday's family counseling "fascinating."

I told her our timely intervention appeared to have had a favorable impact on the Cubans and was flattered that she found my book on Family Therapy, my parting gift to her, inspiring.

Amelia and I continued to provide seasonal fruits, hoping the Cubans would eventually acquire a taste for them.

On arriving home I noticed Geronimo, a picture of the leisure class, browsing in the vegetable garden, cutting weeds with one hand and holding a bottle of pop with the other.

Juana was napping sedately on the porch on a chaise lounge.

The peacefulness existed outside. Inside the house, however, Maria was overly energized as if she were being revitalized by her new vitamins. She moved about vivaciously and, to some extent, aimlessly.

When I showed her the fresh fruits we had purchased, she brusquely refused them, demanding avocadoes and mangoes. I encouraged her to eat some blueberries. Almost as if the tiny berries had a capacity to thrash her she became reluctant to touch them.

She hesitated, generated just enough curiosity to pick up a single berry, and barely broke its skin with her teeth.

"No, no," she cried aloud, dropping the piece of fruit on the floor, "it's too sour."

At 8 o'clock, just as Tim and I were repairing Amelia's tricycle, a white car entered our driveway. It was Anna Stein.

"This is a pleasant surprise, Anna."

"Got good news. The Commissioner's wife in Spencer is looking for a cleaning lady."

"My goodness, we must tell them immediately."

Anna held back for a moment.

"Did Salty tell you about the belt factory? We didn't fill out any application. Twenty people were on the waiting list for work."

"Well," I replied philosophically, "life had a way of balancing out its misfortunes," and encouraged Anna to share the good news with the Cubans who were clustering together on the porch.

Then I rushed inside to inform Amelia of the fantastic revelation.

"It's a job. The boredom should diminish. There is paying work and they could begin striving to achieve their dream house."

"That's great," Amelia exclaimed ecstatically.

"And Anna volunteered to drive Maria to work every morning and return her every noon . . . and she agreed to do it right to the middle of winter."

I hurried outside to witness the exhilaration and joy of theCubans, expecting to find Maria deliriously happy to have the opportunity to work for money.

As I flung open the door a hope-shattering gloom greeted me.

"We got a problem here. Maria does not want to work."

"But day after day she nagged and nagged that she wanted work and now that she has the opportunity, she doesn't want it?" I asked, aroused and completely bewildered.

Amelia was perplexed by news of the turndown.

The time was exceedingly ripe for another family conclave.

Anna was willing to interpret for us but would need to drive back home before nightfall because of an eye condition.

Realizing the indispensability of her cooperation, I gladly consented to drive her home if she considered my assistance necessary later.

It was settled. We gathered the Cubans together and with Amelia, Anna and myself, we entered the living room.

Recalling how everyone tried to speak at once during the first counseling session, I established one ground rule:

"When you speak, you speak one at a time."

Immediately, I perceived Maria changing her seat. She moved from her seat, next to her husband, and occupied a distant chair across from him.

"I want to leave this place," said Maria, mincing no words.

"Tomorrow?" I asked, as patiently as possible.

"It can't be today?"

"If you want to leave, I must make arrangements. Perhaps you will find another home. If you wish to return some day, you are welcome here."

Amelia wanted to know what prompted Maria's rapid decision.

"Because I feel bad. I feel bad because of family problems. All I can say is I have a headache. I want the papers so I can leave tomorrow."

'Fine," I said, "We'll make the arrangements but, before you go, do you realize what you are doing?"

"Yes."

"This is the 9th day we have you" observed Amelia, "and we notice you make rapid decisions . . . and afterwards you change your mind. It can become very expensive to do things just because you want them done."

"Now," I said, "If you go to Fort Chaffee and decide to return here, the trip will cost you $400."

"I'm not going to come back."

"But if you get another family, Maria, you will still work."

"But, at least I am alone and won't have these hassles."

"Are you satisfied to live with Anna, away from the others?"

Juana began whining and wailing, creating numerous, enervating sounds.

"No," replied Maria, the center of everyone's concern.

Amelia explained to Maria that she was in the middle.

"Here's mamma and here's Geronimo," she said, pointing at each, "and you are in the middle, torn by two forces."

I watched carefully when you rushed to the cafe last Wednesday. Originally, your intention was to make supper, but then you were overwhelmed by a strong impulse. Right away you were compelled to move there. 1 mean . . . you don't even think what you are doing sometimes.

. . . and the feeling was that there was limited privacy downstairs: that we understood, but everything was being transferred to the cafe between six and seven. By 7:30 you, Maria, were at the neighbor's crying very hard. You knew where this house was but your wailing came from a great distance.

We saw you carrying on and we felt how torn you were between the two forces . . . but you need to grow up."

"She can't make the decision to choose her husband," I declared.

"We've tried to explain it to her," said Anna, "that this is her spouse and the spouse comes first."

Juana persisted with her excruciating groans.

"I've made my decision," Maria replied staunchly.

"That's fine," I said, "Now which one goes with her?"

Geronimo decided that he should go.

"Is Juana going also?"

"No, I will stay," said Juana, writhing and moaning. "I raised you and you are my life."

"Those two are married, so give them a chance for happiness," Amelia reminded Juana. "We will provide for you here . . . and if Maria and Geronimo wish to return in the future, we will welcome them back."

Juana directed them to go to Miami because a friend there would pick them up and take care of them. "I'll be staying here waiting with open arms and you come visit me every six months. Don't go to the Fort, go to Miami."

"No, I'm going alone."

"But I can't let her go alone," Geronimo protested. "She can't survive alone. She is pregnant, a woman who doesn't know what work is because she has never worked. I can guide her and I can work."

Amelia thought that Maria had the mentality of a big baby and didn't know anything about the world.

"No she doesn't," agreed Juana, "because I was for her everything. I gave her everything."

I replied scornfully, "And you ruined her for the world."

"No, he goes with her; she shouldn't go alone. They prefer to go to Miami where they have friends. I stay here. I don't go."

"Okay, we'll make the arrangements tomorrow with the Social Services, and if Vincente comes, then he is welcome here."

Juana began wailing uncontrollably because she wanted them to wait for Maria's brother.

Juana's hysterical spectacle did not impress Maria who turned away from her mother saying, "I will not wait for him. I will go anyplace,"

"If you want to go just anyplace, you can start hiking through the cornfields."

"I will find someone who will find me work."

"But we have work for you."

"I want to be elsewhere, not here."

"Maria is confusing," Geronimo explained. "She lacks the knowledge, where we should go or how to get there. I could guide Maria except for Juana's interference which confuses her and tears her apart."

Pondering the dilemma we were facing, Anna made a proposal. She could accommodate the couple at her home temporarily.

Since no other options seemed possible it appeared to be an excellent suggestion.

"Tonight you two go to Anna's place and Mamma stays here."

"I'm 'not going'," Maria balked.

"Then mamma will volunteer and Geronimo and Maria will remain."

"Juana goes," Geronimo directed.

Obediently Juana scurried off to get her clothes packed.

Anna wanted to know, if Juana should work for the Commissioner's wife, would it jeopardize her SSI allowance. Amelia didn't think it mattered, Mark Spitzer said she needed to earn $500 a month before it could interfere.

It was agreed- Juana would work.

Anna went to phone her husband to announce that Juana would be their house guest.

In the basement Juana proceeded to grasp everything in sight, them flung most of it back. With a touch of disorientation she moved about frantically from one corner of the basement to the other, stuffing her belongings into a large paper bag.

Realizing that Anna could not drive in the dark, and it certainly was beginning to darken outside, I encouraged Juana to hurry.

I lifted the bag, bulging with Juana's possessions and suddenly faced a formidable obstacle. Her legs planted in front of me with a wide stance and piercingly looking me squarely between the eyes, Juana said defiantly, and in splendid English, "No, I'm not going."

"Well, it's either you or them."

"I'll go," Maria voiced her opinion, standing at the top of the stairs.

In an instant she began stuffing her assortment of clothing into another paper bag as I reminded her tantalizingly, "And there is a job, for money."

Placing Juana's bag near her bed, I lifted Maria's bag and proceeded to carry it outside. I placed the bag on the back seat of Anna's car and held open the door on the passenger side. But it stayed and stayed open.

Maria stationed herself in front of the car, her arms folded tightly, refusing to budge.

Geronimo, also with folded arms, a red baseball cap on his head, resisted.

"We want to stay here," he said unwaveringly.

There is nothing exciting here, but Anna's place is worse . . . it would be too dull," Maria told her husband.

The bathers across the street were alerted by the commotion and were watching our private, twilight fiasco.

Again Maria returned to the basement. She gathered up an armful of shoes, Amelia's gifts, and dropped them at her feet on the kitchen floor.

"No," Amelia reacted, "they are yours; take them."

"I want to go."

"Then go, Anna is waiting."

Maria scooped up all seven" pairs of shoes and promptly returned them to the basement.

Geronimo and Juana went down the steps in pursuit of Maria. I followed, becoming conspicuous by positioning myself directly under the bright fluorescent light at the base of the stairway. On that select spot I gave the group my sternest of warnings:

"Either you split up or you go back."

Juana was convinced of the sincerity of my proclamation.

In an instant she kissed me on my bare shoulder and breathed into my ear, "don't fill out the papers, doaktor."

I lifted Maria's bag from the rear seat of Anna's car and replaced it with Juana's bag.

"And you will have work and make money," Anna reminded the old lady who sat stolidly beside her, as if she were embarking on her first rollercoaster ride.

"And will she be back tomorrow?" Maria asked anxiously.

As the car backed out from the driveway Maria's eyes were fixed on the vehicle. She followed it closely until it turned on the north highway to Spencer.

The serenity of the plantation was suddenly a source of blissful solitude.

Geronimo and Maria were together in some secluded niche where there reigned a total silence. Being hygienic, it was common for the couple to shower daily but, this evening, they had done it with the unobtrusiveness of church mice.

Tuesday, July 15 I called Catholic Social Services and asked Sister Nadine what options existed if a refugee sponsorship failed. She told me there were no contingency plans. They could not be returned like a piece of furniture yet, legally, I was not obligated to take care of them.

In my sober judgment, I could not turn them away. They would become beggars; they could not speak English ... it would be the end of them.

As for Vincente De La Cruz Sanchez, he could not be located. The Red Cross, who initially brought all four members of the family together at the Fort could find no trace of anyone by that name.

If he had already been relocated, they would not know where because he was not identified by name, only by a refugee number. To locate him, we would need that number.

Juana rang Mrs. Carreras six times yesterday requesting help because she was sad and crying. It gave Juana plenty of action in receiver slamming when she heard such impertinent advice from Mrs. Carreras as, "You should be content to have a roof over your head and food to eat."

I told Mrs. Carreras that I was favoring solo experiences for the Cubans and wanted Maria to come alone for her Friday checkup.

She told me of her discussion with Attorney Jensen following our first counseling episode. They scrutinized the evidence and decided: if Vincente's name is Sanchez, which is unlike Juana's then, undoubtedly, she had different husbands.

Also, Juana, the alleged mother of Vincente, had never instigated or even devotedly supported his sponsorship, suggesting that Vincente appeared more closely related to Maria, who did.

Thought was given to the possibility that Geronimo and Maria were not married. Mrs. Carreras recalled that the arbitrary picking of mates in Cuba without marriage was quite a common practice.

Amelia phoned the house and was surprised that Maria answered. Of course, she could have been missing Juana and was frantically awaiting her call.

In actuality, Maria had already received several calls from Juana and was anticipating more.

When Amelia and I arrived home, the couple were showering together.

Amelia wanted some pork chops for supper. Being the only available member of the family within earshot, I was elected to get the meat.

I decided to invite Geronimo to come along for company. Just then, Anna called.

"We got problems here, Juana is threatening."

"Threatening what?" I asked.

"If she can't spend the night there, she won't work tomorrow."

"Fine, above all, don't let her break your will."

"But she's going to walk out. Maria told her this morning that Geronimo cried all night and wants her back."

I asked Anna to lay down the law, to tell Juana that if she comes back, she must leave, that I have the papers.

The instant Anna transmitted my stinging message to Juana I could hear the turmoil intensify.

"Now we've done it. . . she's in a panic. Can she talk with Maria?"

"No, six calls a day is too much."

"Then come over and Help, for heaven's sake."

Before I would drive the ten miles to Spencer, Geronimo and I would go to Teds for the carne.

I motioned to Maria, who was walking beside Geronimo like a faithful puppy, to stay behind.

Seeing us drive up the road she swiftly dashed into the garage.

Being alone with Geronimo gave me the opportunity to ask him about Juana's absence. His effusive "bueno" left no doubt in my mind. Any claim that he was remorseful over the separation could only be the brainchild of a deceptive mind.

Actually, Maria's reason for running into the garage was to straddle Amelia's three wheeler and ride it up the road in hot pursuit of Geronimo. Fortunately she didn't get very far. Being inexperienced, the trike swerved into a gully.

Later, I noticed a pot of beans with olives on the stove and tasted it. It tasted good and there was more than enough in the pot for two.

I asked Amelia if she was in the mood to try some. Since olives were not her cup of tea, there was still plenty of room for compromise: Amelia ate only beans and I went for the complete works, beans and olives combined.

I followed Anna's instructions but overshot her home by three doors. Edward was behind me on his bike, intending to guide me to the correct residence, as Anna and Maria appeared at the door's entrance, impatiently waiting.

Arriving, I felt" like a drop of water for a parched tongue, a last ray of hope, an omnipotent mediator with all of the answers.

"I've run the gamut of emotions," Anna said immediately. "I've passed through every conceivable emotion, frustration, hostility, depression . . . it's getting to me." Yet, she was apprehensive that Juana was suffering.

I agreed that Juana's stress was authentic but there was no way to resolve her problem without passing through a painful barrier.

Anna handed me a letter from Juana. It was alleged to have been written by Jennifer, Juana's employer, beseeching me to allow her to come home.

Since it was written in Spanish and Jennifer's only tongue was English, Anna was positive Juana was the author.

"I wish to tell you doctor, that you should forgive her for her behavior. It will not be repeated. She has been very useful tome. My husband has met her and says she has good principles and everything happens by the grace of God." Anna reported that Jennifer was pleased with Juana's work and was looking forward to her returning.

Though the salary was a pittance, two dollars an hour for cleaning and one dollar an hour for baby-sitting, arrangements were made for one cleaning afternoon and two sitting afternoons per week.

Juana promised that yesterday's scene would never be repeated. If it should happen again 1 would have her permission to kick them out.

Anna explained about her emotional reactions and blamed the compactness of the house and how closed-in she felt in Juana's presence. She was feeling constantly fatigued; there was an ever present drainage of her energy and .', . there was no escaping.

"If only I didn't understand Spanish. If only I didn't have to listen to Juana, then the impact would have been less devastating on my nerves,"

Juana persevered, employing every conceivable tactic, to have me consent to her returning immediately to my home. When I answered, "no," Edward, a usually quiet volcano, flared up. He demanded an immediate decision on the duration of Juana's stay at his house.

"How long do you intend to hold her against her will," he snapped. "We feel that she has been held captive long enough and the hell with your therapy."

Edward was 100 per cent in favor of the Cuban family being together "where they belonged" and washed his hands of this "kidnapping," while Anna was fearful that they could be liable to a suit.

Meanwhile, Juana, seeing the growing dissention between the Stein's and myself, began to badger me with a renewed determination.

"It will never happen again," she pleaded, over and over.

In two or three days she would receive her SSI check, she explained. With the money all three would get an apartment which Mrs. Carreras would help them find.

I told Juana that her assertions were untrue. Mrs. Carreras was pleased to find an apartment for her only.

Unrelenting, Juana persisted that they would all share an apartment .and her money would make it so.

Juana was vehemently begging that I should take her tonight.

I looked at the haggard countenance of Anna and said regretfully, "I would take her only because you want me to take her."

Then, quite unexpectedly, Anna agreed to quarter Juana for one more night.

"For your children and your mother you should take me tonight," Juana persisted, all the harder.

1 told her I was not impressed with her theatrics.

"If you don't take me immediately, I will walk."

I looked at my watch and made a fast calculation.

"The distance is ten miles. It will take four hours. If you begin now, you will arrive at two in the morning."

1 opened the door as a salute to the start of Juana's trek. But she refused to respond to my cue.

Why won't you take me?"

"Because you are a nuisance to the couple and you're ruining their lives."

Juana began to cry and wail bitterly.

"She has real pain," Anna said with concern.

"You can cry if you wish, but you are not going home. I know you are in pain but you have always transmitted that pain to others. Anyone in your presence suffers. Geronimo and Maria have suffered and now you make the Stein family suffer."

Edward hoped they could find an apartment for Juana, being concerned with her threat to walk the ten mile distance.

"She won't do it, Ed. That is a ploy which feeds on conscience.

She is intelligent enough to realize it is a dumb idea. The dramatic pathetic ploy works if you allow yourself to become fearful that something bad will happen. When she instills enough fear in you, then she incapacitates you into doing her will. She is a grand manipulator, a master of the art of people use and people abuse.

But, she only threatens to walk: with that she would be exercising her will and her right to move about as she pleased. But the walking, and the walking in the summer time . . . it's nothing, so let her walk.

Fortunately," I said, "she is not grabbing a knife and pressing it to her throat saying, 'now take me to my daughter, or else.' Under such circumstances, it would be much more difficult to say 'cut your throat.'

We are indeed fortunate that we have the safer option, to say, 'go ahead and walk.' "

Edward called Juana a typical Latin American mother who clings to the children and expects all to cluster about her.

"Juana flitted about, like a bee winging from one flower to the next, in Havana. She visited, all her kin in a very short time. Maybe she flitted around to many relatives in Cuba because one could not tolerate her for very long. But, in America, she has one daughter and to her she has been giving a concentrated dose of herself which she had shared among many in Cuba.

Maria was the weak one of the bunch. Inadvertently, Juana was out to seize and destroy the weak one . . . like a lion devouring a lame goat."

"Why didn't Amelia come?" Juana asked.

"Because she is occupied with other things rather than catering only to you. Amelia has her own family. Do you want to control everyone's life like you control you daughter's?"

Juana wanted to know, if I wrote a book, would she be a nice character in it?

"Not only nice, but super nice," I told her, realizing I was forsaking the truth.

"You are the best mother in the whole world," Anna told her, following my example.

Immediately we observed a transformation. Juana wasn't being changed into a bona fide saint with white robe and halo; nothing so quaint. She was merely crying genuine tears.

"What a wonderful woman you are," I quipped and added, "but you're not going home tonight."

"Okay, I go home tomorrow."

"See, see," I announced with delight, "I gave to Juana what she needed to hear and, in return, she gave me her cooperation."

Then Juana decided to review the evidence of her popularity. It was Jennifer's baby who liked her and Jennifer's husband who relished her principles.

"What a magnificent person, the best in the world;"

Edward could see the pall of peacefulness fall over Juana's ordinarily intense face as she sat back comfortably.

"And no telephoning tomorrow morning. No calling and, furthermore, you will sleep in the attic and keep away the basement where Geronimo and Maria live."

Miraculously, there was not the slightest whimper of protest.

"What a precious lady."

"I only want to do what is right," Juana said humbly. "If I offend you again, send me away."

"You told Mrs. Carreras that you didn't like Geronimo?"

"She misunderstood, doctor, I said Geronimo wanted work."

"And Mrs. Carreras said you were jealous of your daughter's youth."

"I only said my daughter was young and could work hard. God knows I tried. He is my protector; He will guide me."

"What a wonderful mother ... so kind and decent."

Again, Anna and Edward could see the tranquilizing impact.

"Tomorrow at five I will go home?"

"Tomorrow at five, but only to the attic."

"To the attic, yes."

When I arrived home from Anna's place, leaving Juana behind, Amelia greeted me with information about a Cuban dentist in Iowa. We decided to call this Dr. Gilberto De Guzman immediately, inviting Geronimo to speak with him.

After answering several questions posed by Dr. De Guzman, Geronimo passed the phone to Amelia.

Scantling nearby, Maria appeared especially suspicious about the meaning of the contact. Sensing my displeasure with her, she seemed to be suspecting all kinds of unpleasant decisions concerning them.

A redeeming gesture, a token of some kind from me, a gift of reassurance was needed now, telling Maria and the others that all was forgiven.

Meanwhile, Dr. De Guzman was telling Amelia of his interest in expanding contacts with our Cubans and invited them to attend a Spanish mass next Sunday. There they would have the opportunity of meeting many Spanish-speaking Mexicans.

He also advised us that a Cuban colony existed near Minneapolis.

Wednesday, July 16 I visited Bob, the personnel manager at the hospital and apologized for annoying him with my refugee problems.

He listened patiently as I told him of the difficulties I could anticipate if Juana received her SSI money before Geronimo had gained employment.

"She would use this money to hold sway over them. The mere sight of the money could make them vulnerable, especially Maria, to the dictates of Juana."

Bob assured me that he would keep in close touch with the Employment Service Agency, who occasionally sponsored some of the work positions at the hospital, but honestly advised me that employment opportunities were very scarce.

I carried a black, leather wallet, a token of reconciliation for Geronimo, as 1 drove home, alone.

Amelia was on duty that night. I would be anticipating Juana's arrival from Spencer at five o'clock.

I was particularly anxious to observe the reunion of Juana and Maria following their two day separation,

I looked at my watch as I entered the house. There was 15 minutes to go before Anna's anticipated arrival.

After I set the billfold down on the living room table, in five minutes Salty was already claiming it as his sole possession and Vernon was asking whether it belonged to him.

I went in to the kitchen where Crystal informed me that the "old lady" was already back.

"When?" I asked her, being suddenly intrigued by the absence of any sounds whatsoever.

"At 4:45."

I began to mull over in my mind the meaning of the early return. Could it have meant that Juana had forsaken her job as a final act of protest? Was Jennifer dissatisfied with her work performance? Perhaps Edward directed Anna to return Juana early because of her insufferable behavior?

I was not feeling comfortable about the premature return.

Immediately, I reached for the phone and shakily dialed a Spencer number.

"What was Juana like?" I asked Anna excitedly.

"Very, very calm and very relaxed, no whining or complaining." .

. . And did she call Maria?"

"Once she asked me."

". . . and . . . and . . ."

"And I said, 'no.' She didn't persist."

Anna explained that Jennifer had company in the afternoon, the reason for their early arrival.

She was quite favorably disposed to pick Juana up next week for work.

I had taken my usual evening nap in the basement, where it was much cooler.

Everything in the huge dwelling seemed to be intensely quiet when I awoke. I struggled up the basement stairs partially awake. Then I heard it, an incessant jabbering, a low keyed tirade, a motor humming. I squinted and, from behind the stairway, I could see Maria's youthful foot, swinging like a pendulum.

Geronimo was outside, enjoying the three cats, being completely oblivious of the intense monologue transpiring in the basement chamber and how Juana was filling Maria's head with God knows what,

I went to my office and turned on the air conditioner.. After five minutes I turned it off again, put out the lights, and left.

Though I was a few minutes late, nobody had either called or waited. One visit was sufficient for them. It was so typical of couples who sought help with their marital problems, especially during these economically depressing times.

Ted knocked on a big pane window as I passed by his store. He wanted to tell me my Cuban couple was up for ice cream today. He wanted to put them to work immediately but they decided to begin tomorrow.

Ted needed some weed pulling and a garage full of "junk" to be straightened out. He wanted to be sure they were cleared to work by the Employment Agency.

"With an I 94, they can work anytime, Ted."

He was satisfied and asked for two phone numbers in case he needed an interpreter.

He contemplated on using the Cuban couple two hours a day and pay them $2.50 an hour.

Ted wanted me to know of a "small counseling miracle" I performed stating, "We're back to normal; it's a good feeling." He was referring to some marriage counseling I offered him and his wife, Pauline, recently.

At home, Juana asked me for a card to send to Anna. Though it wasn't exactly what she had in mind, I gave her a box of pink writing paper with pink envelopes.

She received the stationary in a most unusual, ritualistic manner. First, she moved her arms about like a swimmer in distress. Then she beat her breastbone until her chest turned a blotchy red.

I really could never place the old lady in the attic. There was no rail to hold onto, it would be intolerably hot and the lighting was inadequate.

Besides, I could not be vindictive if I tried, not while experiencing the pleasantness which was prevailing at the moment.

Maria was peppier.

The presence of her mother seemed to produce an instantaneous energy transfusion in her.

Downstairs, Geronimo was singing an under-arm deodorant commercial, waiting for Star Trek to come on so he could yell to Maria to come see the space monsters.

How extreme that Cuban temperament, I thought. There was either sadness or jubilation, stress or calm, but little or nothing in between.

On the stove dial there was off and high, nothing in between.

Thursday, July 17 Though our plans changed frequently for any number of reasons, sometimes within hours, we eventually arranged for the essential appointments for the Cubans.

Today Crystal would drive Juana in so Mrs. Carreras could accompany her for her physical examination.

Meanwhile, I called Sister Nadine concerning Vincente. She told me Fort Chaffee had been vacated.

If Vincente Sanchez had gone to another camp, it would have been to Camp McCoy in Wisconsin.

Sister Nadine spoke of one other person who had requested a Cuban refugee, a man in a wheelchair, who needed assistance in getting around. To her knowledge there were no other Cuban families in South Dakota.

In view of the meager interest in the Cuban problem, the bishop would be making special pleas to parishes to sponsor man: Cuban families. .

Under the circumstances, Sister Nadine requested the names of my refugees for the Bishop's Bulletin.

"My group is atypical. If others learned of my difficulties they might conceivably shy away from sponsorship. The time is not right," I told her. "Though it is a remote possibility, I would like my sponsorship to be a success story."

Unexpectedly, Crystal, Amelia and I participated in a small celebration at Mrs. Carreras' home this afternoon. We were celebrating Juana's perfect physical condition.

Dr. McDermott examined her and concluded that she had a body of a 50 year old with heart and lungs of a 30 year old lady.

The golf-sized growth on her neck consisted of fatty tissue. It was called a lipoma and required no operation.

But there was more to celebrate about; not once during the afternoon visitation with Mrs. Carreras did Juana criticize the relationship between the married couple. She lauded them instead, mentioning only that they were very much in love with one another.

The table was set for six, including the 86 year old mother of Mrs. Carreras.

Juana was assuming the maid's role though she had on her special Sunday dress.

The turkey, which was being served, was a welcome sight, so different from the rice and beans which typified the Cuban menu.

Mrs. Carreras stated that the rice and beans prepared by them was not typically Latin. It was more like an African or Negroid dish. She understood that the Cubans, as a people, had 99% negro blood.

Mrs. Carreras described Juana as a tough character.

"And she lies sometimes/' I declared.

"I'll go to confess to a priest," Juana reacted.

Then we talked about Vincente and the fact that we needed his refugee number to locate him.

"Maria had that very number," Juana exclaimed with certainty. "It is in her bag."

I thanked Mrs. Carreras and her mother for the hospitality and the turkey dinner. Giving the flimsy excuse that I had run out of chewing tobacco, I excused myself. Actually, I felt tired and needed some extra rest, having lost six pounds since July 4th.

Crystal and Amelia understood that they, with Juana, would return in the blue wagon and I would drive the MG.

Arriving home, I immediately noticed Maria, her belly protruding, pulling weeds from among the ferns which surrounded the garage on three sides. When she heard the car, she looked up, straining to see if other passengers were with me.

"Buenes tarde."

"Amelia. Amelia, Amelia," she cried out, with no spontaneous inquiry about Juana. I looked about.

Maria was alone. Geronimo was not even within sight of her. I went into the house and down to the basement calling his name. Then I stopped abruptly reasoning, "if he were about, then Maria would have surely found him."

In a few moments, Salty and Vernon dashed into the house.

"Did Geronimo work today?"

"He earned ten dollars. I helped him," Salty said proudly.

"Will he work again torn . . ?"

There was no one about to hear my question. Salty disappeared in a flash.

Before Crystal and Amelia returned home, they stopped at Penny's. Juana wanted a pair of tongs but refused to be seated for a fitting. She wanted the footwear for Maria, not herself.

"Maria can buy her own," Amelia told Juana firmly.

Then Juana did indeed sit down for a fitting. When Amelia saw that Juana was accepting tongs which were ill-fitting, clearly much narrower than her own feet and more like Maria's, she decided to leave without making any purchase.

This evening Amelia noticed in the newspaper that the Acme store was seeking part time carriers. Since Maria was scheduled for her second checkup tomorrow, Geronimo could come along and complete an application with Acme.

Salty would be the likely choice to drive the couple in, about 12:30. He would trade cars, taking the MG, and drive to his baseball game that afternoon.

I made arrangements again with Mrs. Carreras, who was becoming an indispensible support for us, to escort the couple to their various destinations.

Friday, July 18 I decided to try some cold Tang before departing for work with Amelia. The pitcher was pleasantly cool but the orange liquid had a distinct taste of garlic and beans. The pots and pans which were being piled into the refrigerator contained leftovers which the Cubans would be reheating for two or three days.

Having learned to open cans, they seemed to have gone on a tasting spree with the canned goods which were vanishing from the cupboards and suddenly appearing in the refrigerator, opened, but hardly used. Between the pots and pans and open cans there was little space for milk, for the baby.

In two days the Cubans used ten pounds of sugar while preparing about three quarts of a yellowish, gelatin dessert dotted with raisins, a concoction which was becoming as common around the house as tap water.

Dr. McDermott called about Juana's blood tests. She had an abnormal hemoglobin. Hers was 8 instead of a normal 14. She had anemia and, with 60% lymphocytes, she could have leukemia. Yet her white blood count was 7,500, a normal reading, which seemed to puzzle Dr. McDermott.

On Monday he expected to have a more thorough blood analysis.

It was not expedient to take Maria solo for her physical checkup since Geronimo would be going in for his job interview.

Salty drove Geronimo and Maria in together where Mrs. Carreras, Amelia and I were waiting. With Mrs. Carreras' guidance Geronimo would make application at the Acme and also Wilson's, where Mrs. Carreras learned of possible job vacancies.

But first, Maria would have her checkup. As she backed out of the rear seat of the" wagon, the white talcum powder on Maria's brown, slender neck was the telltale sign that she had showered very recently.

Margaret Thompson, a brilliant colleague and friend, who lived alone, had an urgent clothes-washer problem and could not find a repairman to fix her leaky appliance. With plenty of practice in repairing my own washers, I decided to offer her my service.

Margaret, a divorcee, had three grandchildren. When the Cuban refugees began pouring into the country she was adamantly opposed, being concerned that anyone could indiscriminately come to our shores, hungry and penniless, and be welcome.

She considered the influx of the Cubans an infringement of the rights of American citizens who would be compelled to support the undesirables.

She espoused the position, "they should send them all back," because the future of her grandchildren would be threatened.

Ordinarily Margaret would be conscientious in lending a helping hand to an alcoholic or a delinquent child. She would be influential in supporting programs for the aged and infirm but, ironically, with the Cubans, she had no trace of sympathy.

When 1 teased Margaret that I would like to bring a refugee family to South Dakota she was amused, ridiculing my intention.

At this time, to the best of my knowledge, she was unaware of the presence of my Cubans. How devilish of me if I came to fix her washing machine in her plush, expensive home with my topnotch Cuban apprentice, black Geronimo.

Again, at 4:30, Amelia and I arrived at Mrs. Carreras' home were we found Geronimo and Maria waiting. The applications were completed but no interviews occurred.

Hopefully, Monday we would try again.

We learned that Maria's physical condition was steadily improving. Because of the vitamins and iron pills, her anemic condition would be gone in another week.

The doctor anticipated the baby's birth about Thanksgiving.

Maria was concerned about the birth because, in Cuba, they did "cutting." Mrs. Carreras reassured her that having a baby was inconvenient, but she would have the best of care.

Geronimo had spent the $10, his first pay, on a new pair of shoes which he purchased at a sale. He also bought peaches and plums for Maria for her constipation.

On our way home Geronimo filled up my tank at the Self Service. He did the job well except for christening his new shoes with an overspill of gas.

After we arrived in our small home town we stopped at Ted's for milk. He asked the couple to report for work Monday, at five.

When Juana learned that Geronimo and Maria would be working she fitfully asked, "and what about «me?"

"You have a job at Jennifer's," Amelia told her.

This evening the Cubans were all very quiet.

Amelia commented that she had not been able to study for her professional exams at all the last two weeks.

Saturday, July 19   The couple slept late today, awakening about eleven.

They were in excellent spirits, pleasant and smiling. Both Geronimo and Maria greeted us with a kind "good morning."

This afternoon Amelia and I planned to attend a Filipino outing at a resort on the Missouri. Before we left, Amelia fried some empanadas, a Filipino delicacy, to take along.

Meanwhile, I showed Geronimo the technique of pumping up a tire and how to use a caulking gun. We left him carefully filling in a crack in the driveway as Maria pedaled the three wheeler up and down the street for practice.

Amelia and I returned home about 4: 30 following some grocery shopping. I carried a bag of peaches to Juana and Maria, both of who were sitting on the porch when we arrived.

First I offered one to Maria, who refused. I coaxed her a bit, reminding her that it would be beneficial for her constipation but she continued to refuse. Then I offered a peach to the aged Juana who reached into the bag laboriously. Slowly, almost painfully, she took one. But then she handed the peach to Maria, ignoring completely the fact that Maria had already made her decision. To my amazement, Maria responded to her mother s overture and readily took the peach.

Carlton, who had strong athletic interests, including a desire to play basketball and football in his senior year, said laughingly, that Geronimo had borrowed his jump rope.

"He used it to tie Juana up while she was reading. He then placed a noose around her neck."

Carlton wanted me to know that Geronimo was in a playful mood. It was upsetting enough to Juana, however, because she cried out as if she were being strung up on the spot.

Maria rushed to her rescue from behind the garage where she was watering the ferns. The hysterical clamor and screening which followed ceased only when Carlton stood in their midst and shouted, "shut up."

This evening Amelia asked Maria for Vincente's refugee number. She never heard of it.

For the most part, this day was routine for our family. The Cubans showered and went to bed early. Tomorrow would be a church day.

Sunday, July 20 At 8 o'clock Crystal was tapping on our bedroom door. "Juana is going to church alone."

Her timing was off by two hours. Fortunately Amelia intercepted her just as she was leaving.

The couple didn't appear churchgoing. Missing a second Sunday didn't bother them in the slightest.

In church I succeeded in being less sensitive to Juana's presence. Perhaps the absence of her conspicuously trailing voice helped my composure.

I could see our presence in church was anticipated by Father Haskill who sermonized about being charitable to emigrants.

After returning home, we noticed that Maria was carrying breakfast downstairs to Geronimo. She told Amelia that Geronimo did not feel worthy to share the table with us.

I promptly reached for the Spanish dictionary, intending to find an appropriate word. Then I proceeded downstairs to tell Geronimo that we were all equal in this home and he should eat at the table.

Later, Salty barbecued several hamburgers for all of us. Geronimo was about to scoot downstairs with his share. At our insistence he did redirect his steps and reluctantly joined us at the table.

I discovered that Geronimo would not even try to ride a bicycle. If he could not ride a motorcycle or a car then how would he manage to travel to work once he had a job, I wondered.

This afternoon Geronimo, Maria, Amelia and I planned two activities: to visit Margaret Thompson and her defective washing machine and to see The Empire Strikes Back.

Margaret was not at all surprised to see the Cubans. Mrs. Carreras, her bridge partner, had tattled to Margaret, ruining the surprise I intended.

At least for the sake of appearance, Margaret was gracious and thanked us for inviting the couple along. Of course she wanted to show them immediately her showpiece of a home. She invited Geronimo to view the two bedrooms she had recently so lavishly redecorated but somehow the communication between them had failed. Geronimo was mainly interested in the location of her toilet.

Meanwhile, Maria was commenting to Amelia that Margaret's home had no flies and she wouldn't mind working in such a beautiful home.

The contrast was striking; there lived Margaret in her sumptuous, lavish, ultra modern home valued at well over a hundred thousand, and here was Geronimo, repairing her washer on a Sunday without a penny in his pocket and probably running short of food stamps.

Though we both worked on the washing machine together, Geronimo left no richer than when he came and probably helped save Margaret the price of a new machine.

It was an excellent example of how the rich got richer and the poor poorer.

A short while later we entered the downtown theatre.

Geronimo chose to sit in the very last row of seats.

In time, I realized what an excellent choice that was for the couple. From the moment they sat down, except during an occasional mouthful of popcorn, they babbled together in Spanish.

Their unrelenting jabbering during the movie was clearly annoying to the people sitting around them. What was more amazing was their complete unawareness of the heads which turned in their direction and lack of regard for the expressions of disgust which literally surrounded them.

I was actually feeling more than a slight apprehension about the couple's safety, especially when certain parts of the movie, which ordinarily prompted a suspenseful silent emotion from the spectators, elicited an inappropriate flow of Spanish gibberish from the couple in the back row.

On our way home from the theatre, Maria wanted me to return to Margaret's place because she left a cigarette behind.

Monday, July 21 This morning Margaret mentioned that Geronimo left his lighter behind at her house and she would return it to me when she remembered to do so. The only other reference she made to the Cubans was to ask, "How did they get on the boat?"

Dr. McDermott reported on Juana:

"No cancer; maybe pernicious anemia," but he would need further blood studies.

Just as we arrived home, Salty and Geronimo were arriving. They were both riding bikes. To my surprise, Geronimo was not only riding my bike, but he was doing it like an acrobat, with one hand, pulling the lawnmower behind him with the other. They had been working somewhere.

In 15 minutes Geronimo and Maria were scheduled to work at Ted's grocery. Amelia would drive them uptown this first working day and interpret Ted's instructions for them.

Though this had been Juana's scheduled day to work in Spencer, she didn't go. She learned from Anna how pleased Jennifer was with her performance but she decided to do her own housework.

At six Anna called, exposing the truth: Juana was making Jennifer a nervous wreck. She would carelessly leave the door open with the air conditioning on. The flies were everywhere. Also, Jennifer would hear her baby crying and Juana would make no move to respond to the cry.

Anna asked if I knew Rose Brail. I did. They lived three miles east and a mile north on the Old Rockview Road. There was a familiar fishing hole nearby where Salty, Vernon and I spent some quiet Saturday afternoons.

They were Fundamentalist Baptists, 1 told Anna and, though we hadn't met them personally, they were know to us as "real good people."

Anna wanted us to know that the Brails were being entertained at their farm by a young group of religious singers who had just returned from South America.

We were to expect a personal invitation from Rose.

Carlton was growing fond of Juana, I think mostly because she selected him as her favorite. She praised him for his captivating smile and told him that, in Cuba, he would be chased by many girls.

He began calling her "granny" and she began calling him "handsome."

Carlton evaluated her as "over-powdered" particularly following her showers.

Seeing "granny" taking a drink of water was a very uncommon occurrence but when she added three tablespoons full of sugar to the water Carlton understood that she could not even drink plain water without attempting to make it taste like a coke

"Good Lord," Amelia exclaimed, after checking the sugar container, "the ten pounds of sugar are gone already."

The Cubans were averaging two pounds of sugar a day.

Geronimo and Maria returned home about 9 o'clock. They worked 3.5 hours and earned about $17. They showered together and contentedly faded into the bosom of their quarters downstairs.

I called Jennifer concerning Juana. She immediately wanted to be pleasant by sharing with me Juana's excellent points but it was the flies which caused a quandary.

"Is it worth explaining to her not to leave the door open or to kill the flies?"

Also, Juana was very inclined in assuming that Jennifer understood her, whereas she didn't and told her she didn't. Still Juana acted as if Jennifer understood completely.

With Juana, Jennifer felt as if she was living in another time period. She could never know if her new housekeeper would do something wrong, such as flip on the garbage disposal and leave it running all day.

Rose Brail called, just as I was preparing for a night game of Softball. She introduced herself and apologized that we had not gotten together on a personal basis sooner.

She cordially invited our whole family and the Cubans to the festivities at their farm tomorrow at 6:30 where a group of Spanish speaking singers was anxious to meet them. I thanked Rose for the kind invitation, hoping that the people at the shindig would realize that we did not have elite Cuban citizens.

These were the poor people and I hoped they wouldn't expect too much from them.

Tomorrow Salty and Geronimo would be taking the three cats in for shots. They would pick Mrs. Carreras up and go to Wilsons and the Acme for Geronimo's job interviews.

Tuesday, July 22 Vernon's bike was kicked and thrown on top of the oil tank behind the cafe. The rear wheel was bent beyond repair.

Lucille Millner, from the county welfare called. She heard that Maria was living in another town. Though I denied the rumor flatly, Lucille would not divulge the source of her strange piece of fiction.

Amelia and I arrived home at 5:30, learning that Salty had never arranged the interviews with the two prospective employers because Mrs. Carreras was not at home.

"Granny" was about, hose in hand, watering some of the rapidly growing weeds near the driveway.

Since the storm door in the front was broken, there were plenty of flies in the house.

Carlton was complaining that Maria was continuing to make too much food.

"Enough for an army."

I dropped by Ted's place where I noticed Amelia's trike and my bike nearby.

Inside Geronimo and Maria were at work. They both wore white smocks band were busily cleaning stainless steel trays and grinders which had been stained during the days meat cutting.

Ted's slaughtering room was next door. Yesterday he was very careful not to shoot his gun without warning the part-time help in the adjacent room. He didn't want them to think that Castro was invading his market so he gave them a couple verbal bang, bangs.

At the sound of the gun firing the couple came running, being visibly shaken at the sight of a slain hog.

Ted had noticed that they were exceptionally silent afterwards. In fact, he thought they even cleaned faster after the shot.

Later, Geronimo and Maria crept over to where Ted was skinning the animal. They were smiling with relief and commenting on how good the meat looked.

The couple's work was very pleasing to Ted. It was better than he expected, even more efficient than his very own cleanup efforts, he admitted, as he leaned against his meat counter, all dressed up for the Brail picnic.

I asked Ted if there were any complaints about town. He knew of two, both of whom wanted to know how many of "those kind" we were going to have around here.

"These are the jewels. You should be glad you don't have any rotten apples," Ted told them adroitly.

When Amelia told Juana that Anna Stein would be present at the picnic she perceived herself as being taken captive to Anna's home once again. It was the only explanation for the barrage of no's which sputtered forth from her mouth.

When told by Geronimo that she would not be coming to the picnic she blessed herself out of gratitude.

We drove down a bumpy country road toward a white house which was surrounded by elm and ash, barriers to wind and winter snows, and saw no one. Then, from nowhere, a young lad, hair lipped, with his right arm missing, came to the door of the car.

"Allo, allo."

We walked briskly in the direction of a pall of white smoke which fogged the tree grove. When we rounded the corner of the house fifty smiling faces greeted us.

Rose Brail, her husband, Alfred, and a group of young people I had never seen before, immediately surrounded Geronimo and Maria. Because of the couple's popularity, I became an instant celebrity, being identified as the one with the Cubans.

With kindness, the guests had awaited our arrival before partaking of the food.

Now everybody was looking at Albert who rapped sharply on a drinking glass and explained that his house was a prayerful house. He therefore, assumed the prerogative to recite a prayer of thanksgiving.

The large, white cloth was rolled back, exposing the succulent dishes which consisted of at least three varieties of beans. Since Geronimo continued to be concerned about his belly size, his portion of the food was small.

Three of the young people, Lutherans, who had recently returned from a Christian teaching mission in South America, continued to converse with Geronimo. This afforded me an opportunity to learn even more about my Cuban guests.

I learned from the conversation that Geronimo loved Cuba and would go back only when it became a new American state. The government had closed all churches there and would not permit the meeting of youth groups. Only people in government could buy cars. Even with money you were not qualified to purchase a car in Cuba.

Furthermore, it was not possible to buy a farm or animals. You might be told to go to the sea and catch fish for your family, but never were you given a permit to do it. All land owned in Cuba was confiscated and each family was allocated 250 meters. Working the land to grow food was meaningless, however, because it was not possible to buy seed.

Because of the economic pressures, Cubans were constantly protesting against the government. Posters saying, "Down with Castro," would appear. Then soldiers came and burned down theatres and any other meeting places.

People left Cuba because oppression worsened. As the people became deprived of their rights they gradually became more organized from one Cuban state to another and would throw bombs. When the first ten thousand sought refuge at the Peruvian Embassy, Fidel opened up the gates and said to them, 'leave if you want to' . . . but he had no idea that so many thousands would prefer to leave.

The guitar-strumming and singing began, each song being sung in both English and Spanish. Immediately Geronimo was stomping his feet and clapping his hands to the beat of the music. The theme was religious and the performers fired themselves up with a holy zeal to teach by entertaining.

When the puppets appeared, even they, to Geronimo's surprise, spoke Spanish. They sang of joy in their hearts and proclaimed themselves to be the "Kindred," The Family of God.

An engineering student from St. Paul was spokesman.

"We are all God's children, being created by God. We are all His creatures because we have the same blood."

Then the group sang,

"We are The Family of God,
Yes, we are the Family of God
He has called us together to be one in Him
That we might bring light to the world."

As the evening chilled the air, the group shifted its location to the indoors. There, in the living room, we saw slides taken by the Kindred in Bolivia, Equador and Peru. As each slide was narrated, it was described in Spanish out of consideration for the Cuban couple.

Finally, to top off the evening, the Kindred sang a song they learned in a Sunday school class near the Lost Temple of the Incas.

"Jesus loves each one of us;
Let's call Him Big, let's call Him Big.
Jesus loves each one of us,
He loves everybody,
He loves my daddy,
He loves my mommy.
He loves my brother
And my little sister;
He loves you.
He loves me,
He loves everybody.

Then we all rose, held hands and each, in turn, gave his thanks to God. There was thanks for friendship, for safety, for food and for health. Geronimo gave special thanks to Amelia and to me.

As I munched on a sliver of watermelon, I asked one of the youthful entertainers about his religious fervor. He replied that he was bursting with joy in the Lord and had to express it.

Rose accompanied us to our wagon. I overheard her tell Amelia that her sister had some extra baby clothes.

In a few minutes we were home.

Geronimo went directly to the television. He would be watching it until the screen went blank, a nightly routine for him now.

Carlton thought he was learning plenty from it.

Wednesday, July 23 Mrs. Carreras called. I told her that Salty brought Geronimo yesterday for the interviews, but she was not at home.

"It was definitely Maria's fault that Geronimo's interviews were not completed last Friday," she said irately.

At the doctor's office it was Maria who begged not to be left alone. For three hours she wastefully baby-sat with her. She called Maria a fourteen year old child.

"But she is so tall."

In Northern Cuba she could pass for an average 14 year old. A twenty-two year old girl in Cuba is mature and self sufficient. She must be."

"But if Maria is 14, then Juana can't be 70."

"Maybe 50."

"But she is wrinkled, weather-beaten and old-looking. Her hair is all gray . . ."

"It is exactly the mark of a hard-working, fifty-year-old Cuban woman," Mrs. Carreras replied, knowingly.

I told Mrs. Carreras of our cultural event at the Bain's.

Even in that setting I perceived Maria as a lost soul. Being with unfamiliar people only prompted her to recoil, to act more inconspicuously, a pathetic fixture clinging to Geronimo's side.

She was sitting and not participating; looking but seeing little; listening but hearing little; experiencing but knowing little.

Even when it came time to clap with the music Geronimo nudged her to do it.

Juana called Mrs. Carreras twice yesterday, complaining that she had no job. She wanted to be rescued "right away" from the drudgery of waiting but Mrs. Carreras would not jump to Juana's bidding for instantaneous taxi service.

Friday Amelia would drive Geronimo in. Mrs. Carreras would set aside all morning for him.

The job at Wilsons looked best. They manufactured automobile parts which would fit in nicely with Geronimo's newly discovered ambition, to repair automobiles.

As we stepped onto our driveway this evening an endless torrent of Spanish verbiage greeted our ears. It was a three way argument being punctuated by the slamming of the front door three times in succession. The Cubans carried the altercation downstairs, then up again and outside to the porch.

I asked Amelia what they were talking about. She didn't know. The words were spoken too rapidly.

"Why don't you ask them what the problem is?"

Amelia glanced at her watch, then calmly went outside where the voices were loud, intimidating. She took Geronimo aside and reminded him that he and Maria were expected for work soon.

The verbal warfare ceased. In seconds, Amelia's trike and my bike were gone.

Amelia and I went to the kitchen to prepare supper. Juana followed, lifting a pan full of beans from the lower oven.

Amelia wanted nothing to do with the warmed-over beans. Her protests had no apparent impact as Juana resolutely poured the beans into a white ceramic bowl and set it in the center of the table with a tablespoon beside it.

After Amelia fixed a small meal for both of us and we ate it. Still Juana's bowl of beans sat there.

Juana was puttering about the sink purposelessly, now and then glancing at the untouched bowl.

"I wonder what they taste like after three reheating?"

I pulled the bowl closer for a taste. I decided they were durable beans, tasting just as they did three days ago.

At 6 o'clock Anna drove in.

Since she was too involved in the current election as a Democratic chairperson she didn't have time to attend the Bain affair last night.

This evening she came to deliver several posters advertising the Art Council's program for October.

Having Anna available, I took the opportunity to have her ask Juana a question.

"Ask her what they were arguing about earlier?"

First came the question in Spanish from Anna, then the answer in Spanish from Juana, then the English interpretation.

"Geronimo threw a bug down her back."

"But you were yelling so uncontrollable, so seriously."

"Can t we play like we do in Cuba?"

Anna found nothing unusual in such conduct. It was routine for the average Cuban family.

I admitted that the commotion unnerved me. Whereas it seemed like a big problem to me, to them it was only a silly fun time.

Geronimo and Maria returned at seven from their chores at Ted's.

Everyone seemed relaxed and Geronimo and Maria were especially in a jovial mood. They appeared more expressive and their faces more spirited.

We often searched their faces for clues about feelings and they searched ours. At pleasant moments like this the artful reading of faces was more common than we imagined. We resorted to this compensation because we did not know each others' language well.

At mealtime, especially, was face reading carried on to a heightened degree.

I had never seen Geronimo in a more playful mood as he interacted with Salty who had received his driver's license today. Holding his driver's permit in front of Geronimo's face and asking him to see his picture to verify the fact that he was a bona fide car driver, he challenged Geronimo to get a license of his own. Pointing to Geronimo's eyes Salty tried to tell him of the necessity to see straight before he could drive. Meanwhile, Geronimo, virtually rolling on the porch with laughter, kept reminding Salty that tomorrow would be his turn.

I knew Geronimo could ride the trike. That was old stuff, only for girls like Maria now. I also knew he could ride a bike with dexterity. However, when Maria approached me and asked if Geronimo could borrow Salty's motorcycle so he could accompany her to the grocery store, I hesitated.

When 1 heard Salty say, "let him drive it; he drove it this morning," I relented.

Soon I discovered the truthfulness of what Salty said. Geronimo indeed drove the motorcycle proficiently and carefully, but he didn't shift the gears.

Geronimo went along with Maria for a distance, then turned back while she confidently continued uptown on the trike.

For the next half hour I taught Geronimo how to shift gears on the motorcycle. Setting the vehicle on its stand, I started it and changed gears as the rear wheel spun around. The higher the gear, the faster the tire would spin. When the tire stopped completely I showed Geronimo the green light in front. That meant neutral.

With his new instructions under his red baseball cap, Geronimo was prepared. He compressed the seat of the running motorcycle with his heaviness, shifted gears, and sped off. Up and down the street he drove, sometimes faster, sometimes slower.

Whenever a car approached from behind, the driver noticed who it was and took special care with the welfare of the only black man in town.

Maria's faulty judgment was in evidence as she tried to slip onto the motorcycle behind Geronimo. It was only a small Yamaha. Vernon, who was twelve, could sit on it comfortably. But Geronimo and Maria, with their bulging abdomens, could never get on together.

Though Maria repeatedly slid off the back, she persisted to squeeze on. It was Maria's good fortune that the vehicle was in fourth gear. It stalled just as the couple were about to drive off to certain disaster.

Later I found some papers on the kitchen table with Amelia's handwriting.

"I like hot chocolate, I like oranges, I use condensed milk, I cook rice, I cook meat, I drink water, I drink milk."

Apparently Amelia had been teaching Juana how to write.

My hot water was a popular commodity for the Cubans. They had an adequate amount and it didn't involve the inconvenience of pouring a can of water over their heads either.

Amelia was pleased to see the Cubans keeping themselves in sanitary condition as Carlton continued to observe that they "go real heavy on the baby powder."

This evening Amelia and I questioned Maria and Juana about their ages. We learned that Maria was born in January of 1958. Her age was 22.

When we asked Juana her age at the time of Maria's birth, our question prompted some intense figuring between the two Cuban women.

"Forty eight," they replied jointly.

Still I was puzzled. Why would Juana, who married at 26 give birth to all of her four children during her forties.

Thursday, July 24 The group is settling down into a comfortable routine. They shower each night and Geronimo views late television. The couple sleep all morning, until 11:30, ride the trike or bicycle in the afternoon and, at the time we arrived from work, Juana is busily watering the same weeds or sprinkling the same driveway. At 5:30 the couple goes to work and returns about 7:30.

This evening Amelia sat with Juana and Maria, paging through a Sears catalogue.

"They're becoming Americanized," Amelia said as I entered.

Every page in the catalogue had a child-like fascination for them. Maria was strong on fashions and underclothing.

They discussed the cost of a small house where all three could live together. They asked about the cost of my large brick home, the cost of Margaret Thompson's residence as well as Anna Stein's house. When Amelia jotted down some figures, Juana gave a loud, agonizing, "Too expensive" and slapped her head with both hands.

They were pleased to know that a trailer home was more reasonable, giving them hope and arousing their ambitions. They would all work together, get a bank loan, and pay for it a little at a time.

It was storming outside.

Maria, alarmed at the thunder, yanked at my sleeve. She wanted me to see the fury of the storm, but I showed little concern. I hoped she would not run to Juana, else her fear would become instantly doubled.

Inadvertently we allowed the Cubans to perform in the most casual way possible, in the same manner they might act in their native habitat.

Consequently the "Amelia, Amelia" sound pressing on our ears, the sound of urgency, the shrill, the piercing noise of desperation, the feel of an alligator biting you for no other purpose than to show you that a light bulb is burned out had lessened.

The frantic "come on" gestures of Maria, which were obvious farewell gestures, intended to uproot you from a pleasant conversation or newspaper, had diminished tolerably.

Though the Cubans continued to maintain their associations by mail with relatives in Cuba there had been no recent mention of Vincente.

Today I spoke with Bob in Personnel at the hospital. He was optimistic about work for Geronimo and believed something might soon "shake loose." Of course, we would say nothing of this ray of hope to the Cubans, realizing how easily they could infer facts out of simple maybes.

The rear wheel on my bike was irreparably bent out of shape this evening.

No wonder Geronimo gave me no cute smile when I patted his shoulder; no wonder he denied himself his usual late television viewing. He did it.

Yet, I thought pensively, this was he who rearranged the position of the couch when I stubbed my toe against it, he who ran to my rescue when the throttle stuck on the motorcycle, causing me to skid and fall, he who lifted the 100 pound bag of cement I tried lifting and he who carefully held the ladder as I painted the window shutters. His pain would be unbearable if he hurt me in any way.

Indeed we had spontaneously developed a deep, unspoken compassion for one another. God, I hoped he wouldn't suffer greatly over the bent wheel.

Friday, July 25 Today Geronimo would go for his interviews, Juana would give more blood to see if she had pernicious anemia and Maria would get her urinary tract checked out because she was experiencing some burning.

This plan, however, did not materialize because Ted wanted the couple at work early. He had arranged with his family to see the Midgets play ball. With his efficient Cubans to help him, Ted was finding more time to devote to his family.

Juana was off early to play the role of the dedicated Cuban mother looking after her child's welfare.

When she came to the parish rectory Father Haskill greeted her. He gave her a Spanish missalette which she set aside.

Since he could not understand her, he called Sister Salvador at the Good Samaritan Convent. This gave Juana an opportunity to make a desperate plea for work at the convent. She gave the name of the former Bishop of Havana as reference.

"When the Bishop left for Spain he wanted me to accompany him but, unfortunately, my visa was not in order."

Having laid what she believed to be excellent groundwork with her impressive credentials, Juana now insisted that Sister Salvador should come for her, right away.

Sister Salvador knew Juana's kind. She was a "pots and pans" person, the type who she had frequently encountered while in Guatemala.

She described Juana as a boxer who gave a one-two punch to achieve her objective. The first punch diverts the listener with a plea of poverty, strongly appealing to his good nature. While he is thinking of how he can be helpful, she gives him a second punch and takes more than he ever intended to relinquish.

Sister Salvador suggested that Juana try her hand at crocheting. There were different Fairs in the state where she could sell her goods.

Juana would not hear of it.

"That would take too much time."

She needed the money   "right now."

I wondered how the grand opening of the Sears catalogue would affect Juana. Now I knew. It seemed to intensify the "Pot and Pan" syndrome in her.

Sister Salvador believed that Juana needed to talk to somebody. She called and shared with me her private phone number and asked to call day or night if Juana wished Spanish conversation with someone. Then she offered to have Juana as her guest for a day.

1 asked the Sister about arrangements to teach the Cuban's English. There were tutors available at the local college.

She considered herself as not best-suited to the task because she felt sorry too easily for the fumbling student and violated her own rule by speaking Spanish. She found the ideal teacher to be one who didn't know Spanish at all.

Father Haskill had a religious concern. He did not see the young couple in church and wondered why. I told him they were late sleepers and manifested no strong desire to attend mass.

"Did you see their marriage license?"

I did not, but Juana said they had papers."

Amelia needed transportation from work and Salty was the logical person to handle it.

When she called, requesting his assistance, Maria eavesdropped on the extension. She decided to sit in the car, waiting for Salty to take her along.

Carlton, being the older, was summoned immediately by Salty and Geronimo. They asked him for permission to leave together and requested help in removing Maria from the car.

"Geronimo goes, Maria stays," he proclaimed.

"Stay here," Geronimo ordered.

Grimacing disappointedly and on the verge of tears, Maria left the car. Then Salty and Geronimo drove off together.

Carlton decided to eat something.

Suddenly, he heard the doorbell. It was ringing and ringing. Thinking that Maria would come to remind him if there was someone at the door, and_ she didn't, Carlton became very curious. He went to the door but there was no one in sight. Then he noticed Maria, peeking from behind the house.

Suddenly she started running toward the blue wagon. Gesturing furiously for Carlton to come, she opened the door and sat inside. Carlton rejected her request by motioning that he needed to finish his meal which prompted Maria to gesture more frantically.

Out of desperation, Maria ran to the motorcycle. Carlton became alarmed. She pushed it off its stand and the heavy load fell over. Carlton ran to her side and lifted the motorcycle off her leg. He placed it on its stand once again and removed the key

Carlton heard Maria whimpering softly when he returned to the house.

Finally, when all of her gestures, all of her demanding, all of her conniving failed, as a final act of desperation, she hopped on Amelia's tricycle.

Just then, Geronimo came into sight carrying a can of coke.

I knew the Cubans were receiving their medical bills. One came today for Juana. Somehow, I felt she was very disposed to ignore these accruing expenses.

The couple wanted Ted to pay them monthly, thinking their salary should be a total and complete gain for them month after month.

Of course, their food stamps would be cut as soon as they earned their first $25.

As for the baby . . . they had no idea what medical and hospital expenses would be involved. Surprisingly, they were not even asking.

I just returned from the Midgets' game.

Ted, stocking-footed, was there, relaxing in the rear of his new wagon with his wife, Pauline. Potato chips, soda pop and sandwiches were on either side of the snuggling couple.

I hadn't seen Ted and Pauline look so chummy ever. They were rising above the groceries and becoming alive to life and each other.

Saturday, July 26 I spent the day a hundred miles away, watching Vernon play in the State Tournament.

Having had about four hours of sleep, I returned home and to bed. Soon I heard knocking on my bedroom door. It was Carlton.. He wanted me to know that the Cubans had been abusing each other.

"They're acting freely, like they're back in Cuba, so we should feel happy about our accomplishments."

Carlton accused me of frivolity and gave me an opportunity to alter my assessment of the Cuban situation. He had gotten the Cubans' "abusiveness' on tape.

After about two hours of sleep, dictionary in hand, Amelia and I played the tape. Then we replayed it attempting, with the indispensible help of the dictionary, to decipher garbled words. With one final review, we decided the story was a familiar one:

"I am Maria's mother and I don't have to take anything from you."'

"I married Maria and I didn't marry you and I won't have anything to do with you."

"I'm going back to Cuba."

"If you're going to Cuba you go by yourself."

"You may be Maria's master but you are not mine. That's my daughter and I'm going to stay with her until I die."

As Geronimo and Juana argued, Maria's unrestrained laughter could be heard in the background. She was not involved in the dispute except as the hapless bait who seemed to receive some delight out of being the cherished prize of both rivals.

I'm a good mother and a good Catholic," Juana went on.

"A good Catholic does not lie, but you lie. You are a misfit who adopted her daughter when she was 14 years old from a lady in the street because your baby son died. Then you latched on to a boyfriend in Cuba and deserted Maria to be with him."

The sound of the two women bursting with laughter was too intense for Geronimo to continue with a mere argumentative tone. He assumed charge of the microphone, determined to be heard, and bellowed. "Geronimo speaking..."

Later on this evening, Juana asked Carlton to take Maria to a movie. Amelia, overhearing her request, reminded her that movie going was expensive. Juana then approached Salty on the same subject, then Crystal became her target.

Juana asked Amelia if she were bored.

"Not at all. 1 relax and enjoy my home and family."

Then Juana placed some ice in a glass which she had filled with water. The ice water was for Maria.

Maria took the glass from Juana who hovered directly over her, as if Maria was recuperating in a sickbed. As if there was absolutely nothing else to do, Juana stood motionless, her hands on her hips, waiting. Then she sighed heavily as Maria drank the water and groaned a sound of approval as she retrieved the glass

Amelia had called Mrs. Carreras. The plan to bring the Cubans for their respective reasons was on again, for Monday.

In the phone conversation between Amelia and Mrs. Carreras a picnic was being contemplated for those who were Spanish-speaking ... at our home.

Sunday, July 27 It is a church day again, but Amelia would not accompany us. It was her duty day at the hospital.

Juana was waiting for me impatiently, donning a beautiful green dress which Amelia had designed for her.

Once inside the church Juana proceeded on her own.

Before I could decide where to sit, she was already half way down the aisle, sliding across 10 feet of pew, and nudging a pious looking, gray haired woman as if she were a dear friend.

I made my move to join Juana just as she was doing some neck stretching, gawking at the missel held by the woman. Then Juana slid toward me, sat for a moment, then slid back to the woman, pressing against her.

Back and forth she slid, reciting her prayers aloud in Spanish. Though I wished Amelia was there so we could hem her in from both sides, the people were tolerant of Juana's indelicate mannerisms.

Most obvious to me were Juana's nervous knees which appeared to give her bright, green dress the jitters.

On leaving the church I waved at friends. Juana waved also.

She reminded me that we needed milk, "for the baby."

Ted was exceptionally relaxed and friendlier with his customers. He was paying the Cubans $40, their week's wages, every Saturday.

He was gratified because the quality of his meat had improved. He had more time to devote to his processing.

Again, Ted praised the Cubans for their work. He was positive that no one in town could do the same job as efficiently.

This afternoon, Carlton and Salty were visiting with granny. "Mi muchacho" she said to Carlton, smiling at him and clapping her hands in admiration. She looked at Salty. Waving a menacing finger at him she said seriously, "you. I don't know,"

She looked up at Carlton, "You, si" and at Salty, "You, no."

Though the day was argument free, Juana seemed to be concocting something. She had ventured up town twice, riding the trike once and once walking. Following each trip she would retire to the bathroom with her cohort, Maria.

This afternoon, just before my softball game, I entered the kitchen looking for a misplaced glove. At that instant, the two women charged out of the basement as if they were being expelled from a cannon.

Being completely oblivious of my presence, Juana sat down quickly, carefully observing Maria who was about to call a long distance number.

She never succeeded with her call, though she tried three times.

Finally, Maria did make a call, to Mrs. Carreras. After a few minutes of conversation, Maria hung up abruptly and, as quickly as both women emerged from down below, they were now scampering to the basement headquarters to reconnoiter.

Meanwhile, I called Mrs. Carreras and learned that Maria wanted a job for Juana. She also wanted full-time employment for Geronimo.

Mrs. Carreras explained to Maria that Geronimo's interview would be tomorrow and there was no job available for Juana.

"No food stamps, no money." Maria complained, forgetting to mention the $40 pay they received yesterday.

Sister Nadine informed me of the one Cuban refugee who came to South Dakota. He lasted 10 days and settled for a one-way ticket to Minneapolis.

She was gratified that my Cuban family still remained and wished to meet them.

After arranging to meet Sister Nadine tomorrow, I acquainted her with the telephoning epidemic.

"You should tell them to stop or you will have them leave."

She believed they had a false dream of America, an America with no boundaries or restrictions, an America where you take everything.

Several days ago, Sister Nadine had contacted Ft. McCoy about Vincente. They' didn't call back.

I called Mrs. Carreras to alert her of Sister Nadine's arrival tomorrow. We would meet together initially but, for the remainder of the afternoon the couple would be in the capable hands of Mrs. Carreras. She intimated that she intended to have an honest discussion with them about correcting some of their behaviors.

In evaluating the Cubans, Mrs. Carreras called them lower class, meaning the millworker and housemaid level. They were one step above the orphanages where they would be exclusive wards of the state. They were even of a lower stature than the poor, who had aspirations to gain an education.

Monday, July 28 Sister Nadine arrived first, then Mrs. Carreras, in her white Ford.

Salty was 20 minutes late, being annoyed with Maria because she had taken a late bath. She wore a beautiful, dark green outfit but baby powder lay in thick patches on her exposed neck and ankles.

But wait, there was no third member. Salty refused to bring Juana along because "she would be too unbearable."

Immediately, Sister Nadine intended to advertise her phone number.

When she learned, from Amelia, that she could inherit six worthless calls daily, especially if the number fell into the hands of Juana, who was fast becoming a phone-number addict, she quickly altered her sharing disposition.

Sister Nadine asked the couple what they expected of America. Geronimo wanted a job, factory work. In America, did he think everything would be handed him freely? Cuban television reported that there was an abundance of work and everyone coming in would receive money and a colored television. However, for Geronimo this was false, a political propaganda.

Before departing, Sister Nadine promised to learn the status of one other Cuban family placed in the western part of the state. Also, she would contact Fort Chaffee once again, encouraged by the news that 3000 refugees, mostly single men, continued to be detained at the Camp.

Of course, there was concern that the remaining singles could be criminals or homosexuals.

Amelia and I arrived at Mrs. Carreras' house this afternoon discovering two restive, pacing Cubans. They were so determined to be off, presumably to work, that they begged Mrs. Carreras to call Salty. She refused to comply, explaining that the gas expenditure would be in excess of the evening's wages. Their anxiety nevertheless, continued unabatedly.

When we finally arrived home, following an exceptionally silent drive, Amelia asked Geronimo if both would be working this evening.

"Tomorrow."

Amelia then called Ted and learned that he was indeed expecting them today. She turned to Geronimo and informed him of Ted's expectation.

"Tomorrow," he replied tersely. "Today we have a headache."

This afternoon Juana approached Ted about work for herself. Then she came to me, with some feeling of desperation, inquiring about her Social Security check. Making no headway, she finally requested a favor of Amelia, to call Anna Stein. Ironically, Juana was requesting to spend a day in the same home in which she experienced her dreadful entrapment.

Afterwards, Juana was bombarding the couple with a volley of Spanish verbiage of such intensity that I knew immediately her vulnerability had been discovered, bared, and attacked.

The urgent call from down below, "mother Amelia," which I had not heard before, was a convincing clue to me that the couple were sticking together.

Verifying my theory, the couple emerged from the downstairs together. They were positively close, a husband and wife team, as they strolled side by side, hand in hand.

During the afternoon visit, Mrs. Carreras questioned Geronimo about the adoption of Maria. He explained that she was not adopted but "given up, like most of Juana's children." Juana roamed about, deserting her children in the process. She had a small son who died because of her neglect.

"Juana was chaotic. She would break things in her domestic work. We argued because she constantly made Maria feel inferior," Geronimo said sadly. "She is killing me and putting me in my grave."

Mrs. Carreras reminded them it was sinful to waste food and, when they prepared their meal, they should not cook more than they needed.

Mrs. Carreras learned that the couple were married two years ago. Though Geronimo agreed they should have a priestly blessing for the marriage, Maria was non-committal. Her blank countenance communicated a profound ignorance of such matters.

Mrs. Carreras invited the couple for a sandwich and drink. They chose to have water only.

When Geronimo asked for a refill, Mrs. Carreras invited him to take more.

"No," Maria interceded, directing Mrs. Carreras to do the chore.

"This is Mrs. Carreras. This is not your mamma." she said furiously.

Quietly, Geronimo helped himself to the extra water.

Maria said she had visited the doctor often while in Cuba. It didn't cost anything.

'The doctors cost plenty here," Mrs. Carreras told Maria for her edification.

Mrs. Carreras knew it was a status symbol for Cubans to be running to the doctor. For this reason she seriously questioned the authenticity of Maria's urinary infection. In truth, Maria's only concern was her stool. It was black. The iron pills she was taking for her anemia explained the discoloration.

"The whole thing was nothing. Maria went to the doctor for the car ride."

Geronimo voiced his dissatisfaction with the pay, being unaware of Ted's intent to retain a portion of their wages for Social Security.

Did he know where the money comes from to pay for their food stamps or the SSI benefits for Juana? Mrs. Carreras asked.

"From the taxpayer, so other needy people could benefit from it."

Geronimo understood.

It is midnight. The couple are quiet. Only Juana is on the prowl, occasionally calling, "mother Amelia, mother Amelia."

Earlier, she did some singing and barefooted dancing to the sound of stereo music, wearing her new Sunday dress.

Tuesday, July 29   Lucille Millner, from County Welfare, called asking if I received her letter.

"A letter did come," I said, "but I turned it over to the Cubans and had no hint of what it said."

"When they get a letter written in English, they don't understand it. Since it is not addressed to us we don't get to see it, so none of us knows what is going on."

"They will receive $126 worth of food stamps this month, less than the original $160 because they were working and earning in excess of $25. The food stamps should arrive August 1st," said Lucille.

Juana was again watering the durable weeds which had grown a foot in three days. She peeked around the corner of the garage as our car stopped in the driveway.

When Juana, who was exceedingly alert and agile for her age, approached us, Amelia and I saw it, her left eye. It was blackened. Juana immediately sensed our concern and cleverly pointed to the porch step.

I turned off the water faucet.

Demonstrating her usefulness at any cost, Juana turned it back on.

After a moment Juana came into the house. She was excited, her breathing heavy. Thrusting her arms about and calling out Crystal's name, she pointed to the utility room.

Crystal explained later that she was experiencing differences with Juana because, on washing the clothes, she did not separate the white garments from the colored. Also, she used the dryer incorrectly. She turned the knob in the wrong direction causing the dryer to run on and on but the clothes never dried.

Furthermore, the clothing was folded in a helter-kelter fashion on one pile. Crystal concluded that it would be too painstaking to teach Juana how to separate the clothing correctly, that it would be best to do it herself.

In spite of their differences, Crystal commended Juana for being "an excellent house-cleaner."

Crystal and Vernon watched as Juana cleaned and re-cleaned the sink basins in the kitchen. When a cup or dish appeared anywhere she was quick to spot it and remove it for instant cleaning.

"One of these days she'll have a heart attack," Crystal commented.

Vernon thought she would go insane if she kept it up.

Amelia suggested that such women commonly marry alcoholics, then they spend their lives driving them to drink.

Amelia told Juana of the anticipated food stamp allowance, hoping it would have a sedating effect. It didn't make any difference.

After returning from Ted's, Maria and Geronimo went to their downstairs retreat only to be pursued by the catlike moves of a tensed up Juana.

There was no working up to it, no crescendo, the argument was instantaneously heavy.

"Mother Amelia." Juana screamed, as she attempted to scramble up the stair.

Someone was pursuing her.

Amelia and I relented and went downstairs, but only at the request of Maria.

There seemed to be no other purpose to our being there, we soon discovered, but to stand motionless, ricocheting a barrage of words which came at us with a machine-gun rapidity.

"What is happening? What are they saying?"

Amelia didn't know. It was too fast . . . but she would guess. Piecing bits of the communication together Amelia decided it was Mrs. Carreras' criticism of Juana's behavior. They argued because Maria called it the truth and Juana disagreed, calling it a poisonous gossip.

The couple were a solid fortress now, being buttressed by the respected, unimpeachable authority of a Mrs. Carreras, not only to question but to attack Juana s competency. They accused her of wide-scale breakage, of lacking respect for us and causing nervousness in everyone.

The Cuban couple spoke with a might, deciding on specific rules to govern Juana's conduct.

First, she should not do the housework because she is clumsy; second, she should remain confined in the basement area to keep out of trouble.

Hearing the verdict Juana was suddenly faced with an intensification of conflict which was tearing her apart. She was over-cleaning because her work, her right arm was being severed from her body.

We tried calling Mrs. Carreras, seeking her potent influence, but she could not be reached. We then turned to Anna Stein, hoping she could put Juana's mind at ease.

"Mother Amelia said you come and take me to your home, now," Juana said, then hung up the phone.

After the brief phone conversation, Juana scooted 'down to the basement, resuming the argumentation with the others. In a while I could hear a different kind of sound, like a board striking someone's posterior.

Juana cried out, facilitating the fusion of words, making them confused, loud sounds which could have continued until exhaustion overcame the participants.

I made myself heard, calling Juana to come upstairs. Thinking there was a phone call for her, she came up immediately. Directly on her heels was

Maria who was inviting Geronimo to come along. "No," I said assertively. Reluctantly, Maria retreated.

After closing the door to the basement I turned to Juana who quickly realized there was no prestigious phone call for her.

She resumed her frenzied cleaning where there was no need to clean.

I hoped Juana would feel relieved, being separated from the others, but she was not. Within seconds she tried sneaking down the stairs again. Only my loud command pulled her back.

Finally, I decided to guard the entrance to the basement.

There I stood, a sentinel, separating enemies.

I did achieve one positive effect, it was quiet downstairs.

For my efforts I was not appreciated. To Juana I was not a savior, but a horrible obstacle. She would use any stratagem to achieve her goal of exacting more punishment on herself. One black eye wasn't enough.

Clever Juana was maneuvering for position, she was pointing to her head. She needed something to envelop her head and, from the looks of her actions, it was extremely urgent.

I began receiving this strong message, "where is this thing for my head?" She was patting it, rubbing the palms of her hand over it and looked beneath her feet for the material she needed to cover it. From her actions, I thought the top of her head would disintegrate if she suffered without it for another instant.

Then, with both of her hands flat on her head, her torso began to gyrate. This veritable belly dancer kissed me on the elbow and, in an instant, ducked past me.

I stood vanquished in that spot until I heard one more slap and one yell and one more call for "mother Amelia."

The only reliable bait that would brine Juana rushing upstairs was a genuine phone call, from Mrs. Carreras. It came.

After I acquainted the sixty year old caller with the evening's embroilments, including Juana's black eye, Juana came to the phone speedily.

"No, thank you, no'* was the extent of her contribution to the conversation. It was enough. Mrs. Carreras could sense the stress in her voice. She wanted to invite Juana to her home Thursday, only to remove her from the pressure cooker.

Tomorrow it would be Anna's turn to have Juana at her home in Spencer, essentially for the same reason.

Wednesday, July 30 Three weeks have lapsed and there was no sign of the Social Security cards.

I contacted Mark Spitzer again, telling him that the employment agency would not activate their files for employment without the numbers. He promised to call Albuquerque immediately.

Juana's timing was precise. When we arrived at 5:30 she was reliably watering the weeds. It was her unique manner of demonstrating that she was useful and, simultaneously, affording herself an excellent lookout position.

Just then, Carlton, who had returned from a day's absence, emerged from the side of a Van. The shout of glee, the rejoicing, the arms flailing wildly, all welcomed him. It was "hi granny" and Carlton's captivating smile which set Juana off into a tizzy.

Flattered by the hero's reception Carlton was not about to notice Juana's eye discoloration.

After supper Anna called to report on Juana's morning visit to her home.

She described her as a pacing lioness. Her words ran together, she contradicted her own assertions frequently and changed subjects rapidly.

She noticed a wood carving of Moses on, Anna's wall and asked the name of the saint. When told it was Moses, she stood reverently, hip out, praying adoringly to the wooden image.

Juana requested a treatment for her black eye but, first, Anna wanted a simple question answered: Why, if she stumbled down the steps did she not sustain other bruises on her body?

Juana, defending her version of the incident, promptly offered to shed her clothing.

Later, both visited the local druggist who recommended ice for the black eye.

While there, Juana told Anna how badly she felt about asking Amelia for soap. Her supplication gained Juana four bars of perfumed soap which she would hide under her mattress, a jar of Vicks Vapo Rub and a tube of Alka Seltzer.

There was plenty of bribery power in the loot Juana had acquired.

Later on, Anna had the opportunity to speak personally with Geronimo and Maria. She was asked to convey a pivotal message to Amelia and myself.

"They wanted you to know, in the strongest terms possible, that you should allow them to go to Miami."

They had a reliable contact there, a man with two businesses. He promised them work.

Anna estimated the cost of the Miami trip at seven or eight hundred dollars.

Meanwhile, Juana was ranting that Maria should again see a doctor immediately because of her unbearable urinary pains.

Geronimo remonstrated that the townsfolk shunned him. When he sat among them at the baseball game they would get up and leave. He wondered if he smelled badly or something, Anna reported. Also, Juana complained that Geronimo, having gone to the swimming pool, was asked to leave and the pool was closed.

Amelia explained to Anna that such eventualities were possible but we had not noticed any discrimination whatsoever toward the Cubans when they were in our company.

Though the Cubans were depicting some ungracious experiences, Anna reported a kindness extended her while leaving the premises in Juana's company. She backed into a ditch and two men came from uptown to help. They were exceedingly friendly and refused money out of consideration and respect for the kinky-haired, skin-darkened, elderly Juana.

Anna emphasized repeatedly that the Cubans' paramount concern was to receive our blessing to allow them to leave for Miami.

The notion was unsettling as I recalled a pathetic newspaper story in yesterday's Dakota Times. Cubans by the hundreds were flooding the coliseum and had to be evacuated forcibly. Tents were used as living quarters for thousands of refugees who had been rejected by their sponsors.

Because of this latest, daring request, the time was propitious for another group gathering. We agreed to meet at Anna's home this evening.

Almost immediately after the couple returned from work and retired to the basement, the bickering resumed.

Crystal came running up the stairs, alarmed that the condition of Juana's eye was aggravated by another blow.

Our inquirty elicited only one explanation: "the cat did it."

At last Carlton, who was standing nearby, became aware of the black eye which Juana attempted to conceal by turning her head. For the moment Carlton's image of Geronimo as most idealized of the Cubans, was tarnished.

As we prepared to depart for Anna's home, I glanced at Juana's sore eye more closely. It was not only black and blue but a sagging fold of skin appeared underneath, giving the face an unusual, asymmetrical appearance.

Chairs, arranged in a circle, were awaiting us at Anna's home.

Along with Anna's husband we each sat down. I offered the familiar ground rule and we began:

"I called this man in Miami," Geronimo began. "He said, 'come on over. We can get you work here.'"

". . . But we've instructed the children ... no long distance calls without our permission."

"We've done it; in all honesty."

Maria talked with the wife of a friend, but the friend was unavailable. The wife advised us to journey to Miami because he planned to go there. He had work."

I asked Edward if he would chance going to Miami on the basis of the information available.

He wouldn't but, being in their circumstances, he would.

"For the sake of camaraderie" he would rather starve in Miami than survive in South Dakota.

While Geronimo promised to work and save money for the trip, Maria wanted instant cash, requesting a loan to subsidize the transportation expenses.

Maria, preoccupied with money, thought of their salary and expressed her disappointment in the money they received.

I explained that Ted had retained ten dollars of each of their salaries per week, that he needed their Social Security numbers before determining the amount he would deduct. But the full amount, the 30 dollars apiece, belonged to them because Ted kept a record of the pay.

Maria described the job disparagingly as "temporary" while Amelia called it "part-time."

Maria complained of extra work being imposed and the cleaning being "real hard." Amelia boiled it down to the question of wanting work or not.

Meanwhile, Geronimo wanted to be given money in proportion to the difficulty of the work performed.

Edward sagely placed the Cubans in "that South Dakota bag, where they won't pay you any more than they have to."

Amelia didn't believe it, at least not of Ted. She considered him "fair minded" because he was extremely pleased with the work and was considering a pay increase later.

I appreciated Geronimo's grievance and the faltering of his will to work because he had but a paltry twenty dollars a week to show for his intense labors.

I told Geronimo a story, a parable of a son.

"My son worked very hard for two dollars in the fields. He was dirty and very tired every day for a mere two dollars an hour. His was a bitter initiation but a good experience because, after that long summer of hard work, he vowed never again to return there and work so hard for so little."

"How many hours did he work?"

"Eight hours."

"Then for the week he earned more money that we did. We only worked two hours."

"But he deserved to make more because he worked more."

"But I'm willing to work 8, 10, 12 hours."

"These are difficult times; many are unemployed," responded Amelia with annoyance. "Be thankful you have two hours of work."

Maria continued to seek quick and easy money, asking about the mechanism for borrowing, "because we can't put up with . . ."

Then she asked about Juana's Social Security.

I cautioned the Cuban's to plan carefully. If Miami was their destination they should determine how they will get there, who will meet them and where they will live.

Admittedly my apprehension about the Cubans' predicament increased because of Maria ... it was she who did the speaking on the long distance call. It was she who phoned and spoke ... or did she? Perhaps Geronimo had become the victim of the connivance of the two women and not the recipient of honest information.

"I would not feel right if you were stranded somewhere," I said, "and forced to beg in the streets and had nowhere to turn."

Edward thought it to be wiser if we received a letter from the alleged friends indicating their concern and willingness to help.

"If that is the condition, then it is possible," Geronimo replied confidently.

"You have been kind and generous to us. You have shared your home, all your food and help, but this is not the place for us."

"From my own heart, Geronimo, I want what is best for you and I will never stand in the way of your making a better life for yourselves."

Maria wanted to know when a letter, sent from Miami, would arrive.

Amelia estimated three or four days.

I begged Maria for patience. "By pondering carefully the wisdom of your intentions you can become more certain or your decisions. If you don't like it in Miami, then where do you go? Because Miami is flooded by thousands of Cubans who have no place to go. They live 25 persons to a tent and the sanitation is poor."

"We have many friends who live in Miami," replied Maria confidently. "Our case is different because we know someone who has two businesses there, a bakery and a Sweet Shop.

"If you know of the familiar people, then why didn't you arrange to go to them in Miami in the first place?"

"Actually, we thought we were headed for Miami."

"But we assumed you knew who and where we were?"

"No," Maria responded curtly. "At Fort Chaffee they didn't tell anyone of their destination, only that our sponsors were waiting for us. We knew Omaha, but we didn't know where Omaha was. Even our brother doesn't know our whereabouts. Geronimo couldn't tell him because he didn't know."

Amelia requested the address of the person in Miami to whom they would go.

"We have a number of friends there who would help us I work. We don't have the number of the two people with the businesses.

This person in New Jersey, Mario, he's leaving for Miami. That man can write the letter. Since it had been eight or nine days since we called, he is probably in Miami already." '

"How will you know where to contact him in Miami?"

"When we call his sister, this Mario's sister in New Jersey, she will tell us his number."

Amelia remembered that the phone call to New Jersey had already been listed on this month's phone bill.

Laughingly, Edward called it "an underground railroad."

I turned to Geronimo and asked, "What would happen if you don't have work there? What if Mario has assured you of a job and his uncle has enough employees? then what happens?"

"We will call him before we leave. Besides, the uncle is old and he will let Mario run the businesses. Besides, we have other acquaintances in Miami."

"Do you know where they live?"

"We'll use the telephone . . .

I can get the letter from Mario, with all the details," Geronimo assured us.

About the transportation to Miami, I suggested a less expensive trip, by bus. I would find out the cost of the fares.

Again, I cautioned the Cubans to plan carefully.

"You must have your Social Security cards and you must have your food stamp allotment. You will receive $126 in food stamps August 1st."

"There is plenty of food in the house and what you need we will buy for you so the stamps will be your reserve if conditions in Miami should become difficult," Amelia suggested.

"You should also wait for Juana's SSI check to arrive and her Medicare card to help take care of her medical costs. She should receive over $300 SSI for the first two months.

You should wait until these things happen because they will be a great help to you in Miami," I advised.

Geronimo, who had been listening intently, asked about the length of the trip.

"Two days," Edward estimated.

"I think I will get a job fast, and Geronimo too," said Maria.

"I'm. going to have a job in Miami and a way of life more to my liking," Geronimo assured us.

"Wonderful," I said. "I hope it comes true and it is not an empty pipedream in Maria's head.

If you ever need a home, you can always come to South Dakota."

"We're very grateful."

"Is everything satisfactory?" I asked.

"We don't feel satisfied because we don't want to abandon you," Maria replied. "You have been very good to us."

"That's because I consider you my children."

"When we get on our feet we will come visit you."

"Then we will celebrate. We will have wine and many avocados to eat."

"We want a little apartment for ourselves and enough food," said Geronimo contritely. "Here, I could not advance because of my inability to communicate. In Miami there would be a future where I can progress rapidly.

Sometimes at the job here Ted will explain things to us and we won't understand what he is saying . . . but that doesn't mean we aren't going to try learning English because we know how important it is."

"Remember," I repeated, "if you give me a letter telling me you will be provided for in Miami, then I will do everything I can to get you there.

We are assuming that Juana wants to go also . . ."

"When she has her baby, Maria will need me."

Again I advised, "Save the money from the work for the bus trip. Then we will wait for the SSI money which can be added to the work money. It should be enough.

My only wish is that you be happy in Miami and not feel deserted on the street."

"We arc very thankful," responded Geronimo.

"You shouldn't be sad because I will come to see you," Maria promised.

Offering a quick summarization, I said, "Getting the papers together and saving your money might require about two weeks. In this time we would expect the letter from Miami.

Are you happy with this plan?"

"Very much," replied Maria.

"And Juana, are you satisfied?"

"I intended to stay with you, but Maria said she would need me for when the baby came."

"And Geronimo, are you satisfied?"

"I am happy in your house," he replied and said no more.

I drove the ten miles East, to our home.

It is 12 o'clock. I hadn't seen Maria and Geronimo so contented before.

Thursday, July 31 Sister Nadine called.

She learned that four, single, Cuban adults were placed in the western part of the state. Two had already departed and gone to California. Of the two remaining, one had work. The other, a woman, was frightened of the approaching winter.

She also explained that my Cubans had an Asylum Status, which was temporary. About January 15th, we would be notified for them to come to St. Paul, the nearest American Emigration Office, to acquire permanent asylum.

Sister's response from Ft. McCoy proved a disappointment. Vincente was definitely not there. When she contacted Ft. Chaffee again she was referred to the Red Cross.

I explained to Sister Nadine that the Cubans had a phone contact and were pursuing the course of moving to Miami. I favored any change that had a reasonable chance of success for them, I told her.

Sister Nadine agreed. She had encountered, in the case of some Vietnamese families, the reluctance of the sponsor to set them free to pursue other lifestyles.

I had learned that the bus fare to Miami, one way, would be $97.15 per person and asked Sister Nadine if her agency would assist in purchasing the tickets.

She said it was not possible to provide the total amount but a small portion was likely.

Though Geromino had neither his full time job, nor independent living accommodations, which was the ideal goal, we nevertheless achieved a plateau of understanding.

This was an opportune time, I told Sister Nadine, for us to publicize. To counterbalance any bad publicity of Cubans elsewhere, we would submit a success story.

Sister Nadine would contact one newspaper and I another.

I called Ted to remind him of the Cubans' restlessness because they toiled so hard for him.

He immediately corrected my reference to "the Cubans" and called them "the future Americans," terms he encouraged his children to use.

It's none of my business, Ted, but the minimum wage is $3.35."

"My counter help I only pay $2.00, so they are better off.

You know, Doc, this guy in the bar was against me giving them work. He didn't talk to me for two days.

I told him they were legal Americans and there were plenty of illegal aliens he could complain about.

'Your forefathers were invited into this country the same way,' I said ... and you know what, Doc? We get along much better now.

Business is even picking up; it really is."

"Why not, Ted, you've got the feature attraction in town, a black conversation piece, doing your work. You ought to sell tickets."

When I encouraged Ted to share his wealth, he gave me a lukewarm but encouraging, "we'll see."

Since Amelia was on duty, I was alone as I drove back home.

This time Juana was not watering the weeds when I arrived.

Instead, she greeted me enthusiastically at the door, her hands fanning the air over her head.

Actually, it was less than a greeting and more an overwhelming desire to show me something.

I followed her, as I knew I must, to the kitchen.

"Off, off, off" then "off, off, off," Juana read, pointing to the stove dials. She was proving to me that she could turn the stove off.

"Muy Bien," I exclaimed, as she smiled at me with considerable satisfaction.

Being particularly interested in the phone call to New Jersey, the one I gave the Cubans permission to make, I asked Juana about it.

She held up three fingers, beginning with her pinky.

Three calls were made, all unsuccessful.

Then I remembered the phone bill which included the one apparently successful call to new Jersey. I found the call listing on the dining room table and inspected it quickly.

Actually, two calls were listed, one to New Jersey and one to Miami. The cost for each call was a paltry and exact, 93 cents

I was mystified. What could they have said during a 2000 mile phone call for 93 cents that could give them such a complete confidence in Miami?

Geronimo and Maria returned from Ted's place. I could see them walking casually from the kitchen window, a quart of chocolate ice cream in Geronimo's hand.

Since it was only 6 o'clock, the couple could not have worked more than an hour this evening.

They entered through the rear entrance, Geronimo pressing the ice cream against his thigh, hiding it from my view.

I knew he occasionally overindulged himself in ice cream but he was also concealing the fact that he had spent some of his hard-earned money for it, rather than saving it for the Miami trip.

Discreetly, I waited a half hour, being certain that I would not embarrass the couple by catching them eating the "forbidden" ice cream.

Then, I went downstairs and called Geronimo's name. From behind the draped enclosure he responded and came forward. I explained to him my willingness to teach him how to drive a car. He placed his tilted head on the backside of his hand, as Juana would do when she wanted to sleep.

Geronimo has another headache, I surmised, having turned down such an enticing offer.

Later, "Maria and Juana had made four bowls of the yellowish pudding dotted with raisins and invited me to have some. I tasted it previously and knew of its intense sweetness, so I declined.

Just them, Juana raised her shrill-laden voice and behaved frantically for an instant. She wanted to show me something, pulling the lid off one of the large canisters on the sink counter.

She was asking for a sugar refill.

The relationship between the Cuban family members had improved considerably. The indiscriminate, loud bickering seemed to be ended as their inclination to damage each other's egos lessened.

The time was appropriate to approach them for their I 94 refugee numbers.

Maria and Geronimo understood immediately that I needed to send pertinent data to Sister Nadine and trustingly turned over the vital papers.

But when I approached Juana she balked, feigning ignorance.

First she wiggled her favorite index finger at me, then elusively went to clean a bucket. After an unglamorous pursuit and pantomimed coaxing, she reluctantly reached down into her second favorite hiding place and retrieved a brown envelope which was folded twice. She ungenerously exposed the corner of the white paper inside, barely enough to reveal her alien number. She slid the paper back into the envelope, folded it, and dropped it back into its hiding place, as if the beat of her heart depended on it.

Friday, August 1   The food stamps arrived, $126 worth.

When Maria and Geronimo arrived from another one hour shift at Ted's grocery, I turned over the stamps to Geronimo who received them with gratitude and an uplifting sense of relief.

Juana's share, meted out by an equitable Geronimo, consisted of two of the six booklets of stamps. She brought her stamps to me for a counting, obviously wishing to have a second opinion.

I counted the seven dollars worth of stamps in each set and handed them back to her. Since Juana appeared to be satisfied, I made no effort to interpret the facts.

Amelia had taken the afternoon off from work intending to prepare snacks for the Arts Council meeting at our home tomorrow morning. It gave her ample time to call the two mysterious numbers listed in our phone bill.

The call to New Jersey was uneventful. No one answered.

By dialing the Miami number, Amelia contacted what sounded like an over-crowded flop house, judging from the extraneous noises in the background.

She asked to speak, to Mario Alvarez. The, man at the other end did not know him. Amelia then inquired about the availability of work in Miami. "Work is hard to find," was the reply.

The man was not interested in speaking with our Cubans.

Crystal was manifesting a kind, womanly concern for Juana. As Juana changed the plastic liner in the garbage pail, Crystal came up behind her and pushed her dress zipper to the top. Then she adjusted some loose hair pins which held Juana's skimpy, kinky hair in a little ball behind her head.

Saturday, August 2 Amelia called the New Jersey number again. No answer.

Again she called the Miami number. An elderly lady answered who did not know any Mario Alvarez.

For Geronimo there seemed to be a sadness that the phone calls were not successful.

Though Juana gave us her notice that they were going to Miami anyway without the letter of assurance, there was no evidence that either Maria or Geronimo wished to be dishonorable by forfeiting their promise.

Tomorrow would be Sunday.

Amelia and I decided it was time for us to seek another direction. We would all travel south 60 miles, to St, Michaels, the church with the Spanish mass.

First we would contact Dr. Gilberto De Guzman for guidance.

Promptly at two, the first reporter came, followed by the faithful Mrs. Carreras.

Geronimo had on his working clothes, pregnant Maria her shorts with her hair up in curlers, and Juana her kitchen dress.

As expected, the well-practiced Geronimo was the self-appointed interviewee with Maria at his side.

Juana's implied role was to sit meekly and not speak because she would ramble.

The young male reporter, pencil and pad in hand, began his questioning:
"How much did you earn in Cuba?"
"Eighty six pesos a month" (a peso was worth 75 cents)
"Was that sufficient?"
"No, I couldn't make it. I made little and costs were very high. This pair of shoes I bought for $10 in town; in Cuba they would cost $90."
"How much food are you allowed in Cuba?"
"Food is cheap but it is rationed. You can purchase only five pounds of rice per person every month, and four pounds of sugar."
"Why did you come to America?"
"Because it is a free country. You can choose where you want to work."
"In your country, did the government tell you where to work?"
'The official tells you where to go and what to do."

"Were you surprised that the Cuban government said you could leave?"

"Everybody was surprised."

"Why did they allow it?"

"Because of the opposition, the bombings and burnings against Castro. Castro wanted to get rid of the troublemakers. On the television they told us we could leave."

"Are you happy to be here?"

"I'm happy, but I want to get a job."

"If you want me to, I'll run in my paper an ad that you want a job?"

Fine.

"How do you like this town?"

"It's okay. It is very calm here."

"Have you been treated right?"

"We've been treated too well. They have gone out of their way. We've been treated like their children."

"Who would you like to thank for being in America?"

"The American government. I am very grateful to the citizens of the United States Government that we can be here."

"You wouldn't want to return to Cuba?"

"No."

"Anything you want to say to the people of South Dakota?"

"We are here and we feel fine and we'd like to work and we hope the people will like us."

"Before Castro came into power was Cuba better?"

"I was very young but my older brothers and sisters said it was like the United States before Castro. If we wanted to buy something we could buy it. We had freedom."

Juana was asked if she were sad to leave Cuba, after 70 years. "Yes," she replied, "but life is so hard there."

"We thought the revolution would bring more prosperity it only brought communism," Geronimo explained.

"It is dangerous to live in Cuba?"

"Yes, there is danger. If you don't do exactly what you're told, you're in trouble."

"Do they shoot people in Cuba?"

"Oh, yes."

"Were any of your friends executed by firing squad?"

"No, but my cousin and brother were in jail in 1968 for four years for political reasons."

"How was the boat trip across?"

"The boat, that was made for one hundred, the government put 250 on. It was very crowded."

"How long did it take?"

"Eighteen hours. It was 90 miles."

"Where did you land?"

"Key West. We went by bus to the airport, then by air."

"How was the camp in Arkansas?"

"It wasn't very good. There were a lot of bad people who came across, but a lot of good people too. The bad people caused a lot of trouble."

"How do you like the weather here?"

"It's not bad, like in Cuba. Sometimes it is warm here, sometimes cool."

The interview was over. We decided to use uptown as background for the picture taking. Specifically, we would pose in front of the town's nucleus, "Ted's Groceries," signifying town solidarity and support of the Cuban refugees.

Amelia was preparing an afternoon meal. A ham was cooking as well as a pot of Christian rice, Maria's contribution. With a plate of their own cooked food on the table, how could the Cubans refuse to dine with us? Breaking with tradition, each might go a step further and taste some of the American dishes.

Meanwhile, I called Dr. DeGuzmen who had been in Miami recently visiting relatives. For the moment, he was occupied and invited me to call later.

A half hour prior to the anticipated arrival of the second newsman, the young Cubans casually headed uptown.

At four o'clock, the official appointment time for the interview, they were unavailable.

The Steins, the first of the arrivals, were visiting Amelia in the overheated, ham-scented kitchen when a middle aged woman presented herself at the door.

"Yes," f answered her first query, "this is the right place."

As I escorted her to the kitchen the woman reporter presented a broad, amicable smile which seemed to linger perpetually.

Following the introductions, the guests moved to the living room. In excess of one hour we conversed without the presence of the Cubans.

We seemed to have run out of fresh material and bantered around second hand information for the third time when Juana came into view. She consented to join us but announced that she would refuse to answer any questions.

The formality, the newsperson, the limelight contributed to Juana's hesitation. Besides, it was a touchy role, to be relinquished to the skills of Geronimo alone.

Anna had another interpretation. She portrayed Juana as too frightened, too suspicious to offer her inimitable opinions because free speech was banned in Cuba.

"Poor thing," Anna remarked, with pity, "she thought in America she would go to jail if she spoke something wrong."

"Poor thing," I said, "she thought she was still in Cuba."

When the group settled at the dinner table, including the lady reporter, I could vaguely hear Juana's voice somewhere in the house. There was enough Spanish conversation to give me the clue that Geronimo and Maria had returned through the rear, alcove entrance.

As the group began to dine the head chair, reserved for Geronimo, was conspicuously empty.

After showering, he and Maria finally made their entrance, with Juana tagging behind.

The trio were not only presentable, they could have passed for master and mistress of the plantation.

Geronimo was clean-shaven and wearing a pastel-green embroidered shirt. Maria's curlers were out and she wore her bright, green dress, slight makeup and no baby powder in sight. Juana had on a two piece, yellow suit with a red ribbon in her hair.

None of them refused to be seated and none refused to participate fully in the dining.

As Anna introduced a prayer of thanksgiving, Geronimo motioned to Juana to stop eating.

The rapport between Geronimo and the female reporter was magnetic. She knew the art of interviewing well and had just the right type of glamour and smile, a charisma to match Geronimo s on a very good day.

"What would you be doing in Cuba at this moment?"

"Sitting in my apartment, watching television, or standing outside looking at the people go by."

"And where would the people be going?"

"To shopping centers, to the beach, to visit friends."

"And how often do you shop?"

"Every six months. We had special books with coupons inside. When our date was due, we'd take the books to do our shopping. It was Castro's way of governing."

Was there enough to buy?"

"If it was Maria's date to go shopping, chances were good that most of the choice merchandise was picked out. But, if she was fortunate, and they had recently restocked, them more would be available for her to choose from.

Fidel Castro and his 12 governors are the privileged. They and the communist-party rulers get the best goods."

"Are you far enough away from Castro?"

"Up until now I'm very satisfied and I am going to continue to be ever happy being away from Castro. I have found here what all Cuban refugees have found . . . freedom."

"And what does freedom mean to a Cuban refugee?"

"A country like the United States. It is a country where, if I want an automobile, I can get an automobile. If I'm going to give a radio to my baby who is going to be born, I can do it.

All I need to do is work.

In Cuba, it is said, the United States is the end of the earth. It means you look no further than the United States where all ideals can be fulfilled. This is the best there is."

"You realize, Geronimo, we too go through many problems to achieve our dream?"

"I understand that. All Cubans understand that. What we seek does not fall from the sky. Everything must be sought and achieved by ones own efforts.

In Cuba we worked and we had nothing."

"And who benefits?"

"The government. All the factories, the hospitals, the farms belong to the government. We do the work, we give it to the government and then we must buy it back from the government.

The work is harder than in any other country in the world."

"Why do the people tolerate it?"

"In Cuba there is terror, but slowly the people are losing the fear of rebellion. There have been uprisings and many, many strikes in work centers."

"Did you participate in any strikes?"

"In some, but there is grave danger in open rebellion. Secretly, I put a big sign here and there.

I came to the United States because, in Cuba, I couldn't live any more. I was being spied on and could hardly leave my home because my family had never supported the Castro government.

In Cuba, if a person is a political prisoner, his family is so thoroughly watched that their life is made intolerable."

"Do you feel safe in America?"

"Here, yes, I feel secure. Already, when I was on the boat, a North American boat, I immediately felt secure because I was with the Americans, my people."

"What did you know about the American Government?"

"Castro controlled radio and television in Cuba.

They would tell lies about how they would humiliate black people in this country. Ninety percent of the people in Cuba knew these were lies.

I knew because I listened to the Voice of America with friends who were also against the Cuban government. We would meet secretly and talk about the American system.

I was most convinced that Castro was a tyrant when he permitted the poor Cubans to leave Cuba and then would unleash wild dogs to bite them as they waited to embark."

"What possessions did you bring with you?"

"We brought only the clothes on our backs.

I have this chain here, with a cross. I smuggled this out by hiding it in my hair.

My mother gave it to me before I left."

"It must be very special to you?"

"I was risking a great deal. They searched us so thoroughly. We had money and they took every penny. Everything we now have comes from Amelia,"

"Did you have difficulties coming from the island?"

"We were in the waters of Mexico and there was a horrible noise."

"We felt we were doomed." Juana interjected.

"But ours was a lucky boat," said Geronimo. "We got through, but many boats sank. Thanks to the helicopters and the American Coast Guard, they saved many lives."

"What is the population of Cuba?"

"Before the refugees came, ten million. Now there must be nine million left."

"What will happen to Cuba with so many leaving?"

"Those who remain, for many different reasons, will suffer."

"Is leaving home making you feel sad?"

"Yes, I am sad because I'm sad for Cuba. It is a land where I was born.

Unfortunately it has a government with a tyrant, not a president like Carter who gives freedom to the people."

"What do you expect to contribute to the United States?"

"I will give what I can. I would even serve the United States to go to Cuba to do something about Castro. I am prepared to go if there is a Cuban invasion as a soldier. I will take whatever orders the U. S. Government will give me."

"The government can't force you."

"Yes, this is a free country, but if there is any order asking for volunteers to go to Cuba to get Fidel out of Cuba, I would go out of my free will to do that."

"Do you hope to have a baby boy or a girl?"

"A boy."

"Can I take a picture?"

"You can take a thousand pictures, if you want."

I can only take twenty."

"That was just a suggestion," said Geronimo, smiling charmingly.

The lady reporter carefully inspected Geronimo's profile concluding, "He looks" like Mohammed Ali."

The expose was over. Soon the Cuban saga would unfold in the homes of South Dakota Americans.

While Edward, Anna, Amelia and I succumbed to the informality which characterized our being alone Geronimo, who received a sovereign's level of respect for one afternoon, disappeared briefly.

His return with a piece of paper was unanticipated, arousing instant curiosity. At arm's length he held a photograph which he clipped from a magazine.

"I know this man," he said with absolute certitude. "He lived three doors from me."

It was Albert Einstein.

"He's dead," Anna said.

"No, he's alive . . . it's the same man."

Coincidentally, almost as if he were mind-reading, Geronimo mentioned Dr. DeGuzman's name at the very exact instant I was remembering to call him back.

I was mystified because the Einstein drama, then this extra sensory phenomena occurred one after the other.

Though there was a spookiness about these concomitant events, I preferred to believe only that Geronimo and I were somehow synchronized . . . and for the better. I wanted to believe that subconsciously he was helping me to help him.

A successful phone contact was soon made with Dr. DeGuzman who elaborated on the street directions to St. Michael's.

Though he would not be in attendance at the 12:30 mass, his kind invitation for us to become acquainted at his home was appealing and acceptable.

Dr. DeGuzman, eyewitness to the Cuban tragedy in Miami, enlightened me on conditions there: Any Cuban who had no secure quarters, who wandered about aimlessly and had no monetary resource was taken into police custody, he said. Such vagabonds were initially retained in a secure compound in Miami but recently the procedure was altered. Now they were being returned to their basic camp, at Fort Chaffee.

Then Dr. DeGuzman shared his authentic, personal observations in convincing detail with Geronimo who listened apathetically and with a tight lipped Maria who appeared stoic as she pressed the piece of metal against her ear.

The lightheadedness, the social frivolity, blended with proper decorum, had given way to a phlegmatic solitude which, surprisingly, dissipated rapidly.

The number of Spanish speaking residents who lived in the vicinity of St. Michael's was approximately five thousand, the doctor estimated, but practically all were of Mexican origin.

In the entire area there lived only two Cuban families, Dr. DeGuzman's and one other.

Following the departure of the guests, the Cubans were exceptionally jovial, as if they were suddenly released from years of bondage under a tyrannical dictatorship.

They talked with gaiety and laughed with pleasure as the intoxicating mood of lightheartedness pervaded every nook on the plantation.

The dancing spirit of Maria and Juana possessed them to seek out Amelia. With juvenile ecstasies they escorted her, arm in arm, to the hiding place of the polaroid. They wanted to giggle and gloat and laugh ridiculously at themselves.

Amelia readied the camera for her first exposure as the two women deliberated: where should they stand? By the tree or by the bush.

When it was Juana's turn to have her picture taken, she stood erectly, her bulging lymphoma prominently in view, in front of the evergreen beside the porch.

Just at the instant of the flash Maria disruptively bolted in the direction of Juana. She approached her like a matron about to search a prisoner, reached deep down the front of her dress, and yanked out one, two three dishtowels.

"Now, go ahead."

Sunday, August 3   With the sky blackening in the West, we departed in the spacious, blue wagon. I stopped for gas.

Geronimo got out promptly. Having had one prior experience at filling the gas tank he wanted to improve on his expertise and, simultaneously, show his gratitude in small ways.

The rain struck at the car in sheets, hitting us broadside, as we headed Eastward.

Out of fright Maria squeezed tightly under Geronimo's deformed arm.

In two hours we arrived at our destination on this drenched and dreary day, a day hardly suitable for a sabbath.

After swerving the car precisely next to the curbstone I glanced at the steeple of St. Michael's, a short distance down the road . . . Then I noticed, in my side view mirror, that the metal flap over my gas tank was up.

"Oh, no."

I left the car flustered and, with a cursory inspection, realized that the worse of my suspicions was corroborated. The gas cap was gone.

It was incredulous to think a car could run on water but I had the strongest hunch that I would be finding that out soon.

There were numerous Mexicans milling about in small clusters at the entrance of the church.

With the exclusiveness of spoken Spanish and the complete absence of English, I envisioned myself as helpless, lost in a foreign country in the middle of mid America as we walked a gauntlet of short people.

Though mass was beginning, most of the people were outside, not within. Before it ended, however, they would extirpate themselves, one at a time, and trickle down the sides of this aged house of worship.

I estimated that 50% of the Mexicans who came to church never crossed the portals, remaining at the primary group stage. They stood and stood and talked long enough, then departed and called their obligation fulfilled.

The church was half full at the last blessing.

Women, with long black hair flowing down their backs had a high representation ratio along with multitudes of children who cavorted about the pews.

The first and only song was the Battle Hymn of the Republic sung in Spanish without the benefit of a choir. The sound emanated from an excessively harsh, scratchy recording.

The priest was Father Ramos. Amelia knew him from several pot luck parties we frequented at one resort or another on the Missouri.

Following mass we approached him at the church door where he availed himself to the departing churchgoers, He shepherded a flock of a hundred Spanish speaking families in his congregation, he told us.

I turned to Geronimo and suggested that this might be the type of place he would like to call home.

He was agreeable, especially if he had work.

Father Ramos referred him to the local meat-packing plant and its new annex for which additional workers were being recruited.

I asked if Geronimo would be penalized because of a language barrier. Father Ramos called it "no problem," not when 70% of the employed were Mexicans.

Father Ramos then introduced us to a short, obese woman, Mrs. Margarita Rigga.

Mrs. Rigga, a church leader, motioned us to come with her.

We paraded into a large, quiet room with a long window in the rear of the church.

Just as we positioned several chairs in a circle, a lean man with a mustache began to squeeze through the partially closed door.

"Pepito, come in."

It was Margarita's husband, Peppi, a sixteen year veteran at the meat plant.

We soon learned, to the Cubans' delight, that a worker could earn $5 an hour and some unoccupied houses were available on the grounds.

On August 11th, in one week, the new annex would be ready for operations and tomorrow the taking of applications would begin.

Though it was inactive on a Sunday, Peppi decided to show us the exterior of the sleeping giant, a white structure spread over several acres, three miles from the town's boundary.

The employment building was small, but conspicuous by comparison, because it stood in the forefront, with a wire fence enclosing the huge plant in the background.

I parked behind Peppi's Volkswagon beside the locked building. There was obviously little to do except step in water puddles at that abandoned spot, so Peppi and I decided to take a peek through the window at a batch of application forms and six long tables.

We drove in a semi-circle to the rear of the plant where we whiffed a foul, decaying odor.

A village, constructed of cement blocks and painted white, a mirage on the plain, beckoned us.

By twos I counted 48 of the large, box shaped structures as we moved slowly down the ruler-straight, dusty, main street which formed a loop at its terminus.

Visible among the corridor of dwellings were inhabitants of short stature with yellowish skin color, jet-black hair and protruding cheek bones.

The acquisition of housing was possible, Peppi informed Geronimo but, on closely examining the houses, I determined a minimum of 60% were uninhabitable. They were being used as giant storage bins.

Peppi remained optimistic, intending to make a formal request for a rental property at the appropriate time, the time of job application.

Fifteen, sixteen years had transpired since they lived in that improvised, repetitively-styled hamlet, Peppi and Margarita reminisced. With washer, dryer, refrigerator, stove and grounds maintenance, they bedded down there for five years, contending with the odor of the factory, for $22 a week.

Peppi raised heavenward the hopes of Geronimo, suggesting that the women not be spared this grand opportunity for work.

Margarita advised us, in her motherly, concerned fashion, to rise before the break of dawn and be in the protruding building with the stack of application forms and rows of tables by eight o'clock. In her sluggish, drawn-out manner, she charitably offered her services as general advisor and interpreter for this momentous occasion.

Whatever time we set foot on her doorstep, that was the propitious moment. She would be available.

We tailed the Mexican couple's Volkswagon the three miles distance to their house where middle-aged Peppi humbly disclosed that it wasn't paid for.

According to my Timex it was 3 o'clock, the time of our appointment with Dr. DeGuzman.

My indispensible map on my lap, I focused on the X mark, our destination. Twenty nine city blocks lay ahead, barring any unforeseen delays.

We bid Peppi and Margarita Rigga "adios" and sped off northward.

Thirty five minutes later, after some minor map reading errors, we arrived at a hilly slope beneath Dr. DeGuzman's home which perched like an eagle's nest above us. We ascended skyward up an endless stairway of concrete slabs to the front porch.

A brass plaque, positioned beneath the doorbell read, "Dr. Gilberto DeGuzman."

He was expecting our arrival and took the initiative of inviting the only other Cuban resident in the area, his friend, Dr. Guido, a professor of Spanish and French at a local college.

Mrs. DeGuzman, a thoroughly ivory-skinned woman, was prepared to be ingraciating to a superlative degree to the dictator- abused wayfarers. Juana diligently detected the magnanimous concern and felt spontaneously attracted to the woman of DeGuzman house.

A 1978 edition of outstanding Cuban Socialites, which came to Juana's attention, aroused her curiosity and served to cement the intensifying relationship between the two women.

Juana gleaned through the pictorial pages with Mrs. DeGuzman with an insatiable thirst.

With an unquenchable desire to be identified with the elite, Juana began to swear, on her mother's grave, that she had found the Miami address of the millionaire godparents of Maria in the book.

She convinced Mrs. DeGuzman that she had found her dream opportunity, to gain employment as a housekeeper in Miami with this renown family in whose employ she spent seven- teen years in Cuba.

Events appeared to be fitting miraculously into place and Mrs. DeGuzman began feeling that hers was a prominent role in the shaping of a prosperous future for Juana. Under these promising circumstances what could Mrs. DeGuzman do but perform one final act of generosity, by giving in to Juana's request to call the Miami number.

Meanwhile, Geronimo, with one eye trained on the resourceful Juana, was exchanging viewpoints with the ruddy-faced, rapid-speaking Dr. Guido who habitually slapped him on the knee as they conversed.

Amelia and I spoke with Dr. DeGuzman, who informed us of two other Mexican colonies in nearby towns.

He told us that Castro sent to America an entire school of 75 deaf and blind children along with their teacher. Also, a group of gays in California offered to sponsor all of the homosexuals in Fort Chaffee.

Women acted as prostitutes so they could come to America and men faked homosexuality.

After about a half hour Geronimo, in an unbecoming, stern voice called for an immediate departure. Responding to Geronimo's insistence that we leave, we prematurely exchanged farewells at the door. Dr. Guido thanking me profusely for helping the Cubans since he, too, 17 years earlier, was a Cuban refugee from the Bay of Pigs episode.

Quietly, he whispered in my ear what Geronimo told him: "In order to leave Cuba, Vincente pretended to be a homosexual."

Halfway home I invited the Cubans to dine. None accepted.

Shortly after arriving home I could sense a problem.

Geronimo was outside, standing pensively, watching the gathering storm clouds. When he returned to the house he squeezed a note into my hand for Amelia.

Unable to understand the writing, Amelia called Anna.

The note explicitly told us to forbid Juana from leaving the house. Unless we abided by his wishes, Geronimo would leave.

We were faced with another problem, Anna agreed. She and Edward promised their immediate assistance.

The Steins arrived just ahead of the storm.

We gathered together and settled in the living room.

"I beg you a thousand times, take Maria and I anywhere, but don't take Juana until she can behave. Juana talks superfluously without a base.

Today, while we were visiting the DeGuzman family in their home, she talked so much she made me suffer. She humiliated me, and Maria too.

Every time when we go any place we tell her: 'don't talk until you are asked to talk.'

Juana should leave the house only if it is urgent, to visit a doctor, Since she doesn't pay attention to me, you must tell her not to leave."

"Excuse me, excuse, me," Juana blurted out in an urgent, agitated state, them proceeded to speak erratically.

"See, see. See how she wants to say things that have nothing to do with the subject.

It's not because she is a bad person, but she's in a nervous state right now. Her brain is like that of a child. That is why it wouldn't be advisable to take her when you ask us to visit somewhere."

"You and Maria may make that decision, Geronimo," I suggested.

"She's a human being who doesn't reason. If someone tells her about her unreason, she declares she will refrain, but, without fail, she does it again.

Because the friends we visit like our company, they won't speak about her rambling and ... I suffer for this."

"Maybe it really isn't necessary to suffer, Geronimo, because she can't be blamed?"

"She refuses to recognize her own mistakes. Then she is offended when I call her attention to it... we do it for her own good."

"But she really can't help it. If she could help it she would correct herself."

"Excuse, excuse," Juana intruded, breathing heavily. "I have found the address of the woman I sought, I will write to her and will visit there alone."

Before I was desperate because I could not get that address, desperate because I could not find the connection. That is why Geronimo saw me acting foolishly as I did . . . and know this: Did anyone complain about me? Did Mrs. DeGuzman complain because I had the honor of using her telephone? If she complained, then I will ask for an apology.

You must take me to see her immediately."

"No, it is too far," I replied tersely.

"I've got her phone number. One call and she will hasten to pick me up."

"You cannot phone without permission."

"No, I won't call . . . I'm going to write her a letter."

I have made Geronimo and Maria suffer a lot. When I return to Cuba I will tell my children how I made Geronimo suffer.

Be assured that I'm going to be obedient from now on.."

"Juana can't succeed on her own. We are the only family she has." '

"When she says she wants to be on her own, she wants you and Maria to feel sorry for her ... it is her technique," I interpreted.

"No, no, no, no, I don't need anybody to feel sorry for me. I'm strong and I can work."

"Sometimes that is true. When we speak a bit harshly to her she pretends she is crying. If she would reason she would know we do it for her betterment.

Can you see, in her condition she could never survive alone in the United States. It is why we nag her. She gets all upset and imagines she is going to die. . .she has no gratitude."

Juana tried another "excuse me" but Geronimo vetoed it, saying, "Maria goes one or two days without eating but Juana doesn't get concerned. She eats like a glutton . . . and that is why, like a child, she must be punished and should not be permitted out of the house."

"Excuse me, excuse me. Not even in my grave am I going to forgive you.
I am going alone. I'm going to lead my own life."

"When we come together like this and our feelings emerge, then Juana wishes me all sorts of terrible things.

Let her leave the house only with sickness, to the doctor."

"I will go to church every day."

"If you are not at home, let your children contain her."

"For me you're dead."

"In spite of your nervousness, we still like you," said Amelia.

"Thank you. I worked for 12 years. I will show Geronimo who I am. I'm leaving. I am leaving but not with Geronimo. I am going alone.

With my daughter I am not angry. If she wants something, she needs only to write me.

If they go, they're going alone. I'm not going with him."

"I would appreciate it if you would ask Juana to refrain from telling people that she will support Maria because I will.

What are they to think when they hear her saying such non-sense?"

"Excuse me, Geronimo, I am doing that because she is my daughter."

"When you go visiting, Geronimo, I prefer that you decide who comes along."

"Me and Maria will decide."

"No, no, no, no. no. You two go alone I'm not going. . . and even if he asks for my forgiveness. I won't give it.

I will sleep upstairs.

I'll wait two days, then I'll see Sister Salvador and do whatever she advises.

I give you my solemn word that I will never . . . I'm not moving to the attic. Before that I will be on an airplane.

I'm not going to bother him at all. If he's here, I'll be there.

Be assured, he will never complain about me again. Before that happens, I'm going back to Cuba.

I've made my daughter suffer and Geronimo, such a good man."

"But a minute ago-you were saying bad things about him."

"No, no, no, no, no. As long as I am away from him I agree with everything.

I made my daughter suffer a lot and, if I'm not supposed to touch anything, then I won't touch anything."

"I know you two have given us privileges in the house as if we were your children, but I am a person who doesn't like to touch things without having permission in advance.

Sometimes Juana touches things and tells Maria that Amelia gave her permission, but it's a lie. Then Maria touches it because she thinks Amelia has approved.

Juana should not be allowed in the refrigerator without your permission or touch any food."

"Didn't I ask you if I can fix orange juice, mother Amelia?

When I am in my home in Miami, Maria can visit me anytime, bur Geronimo can't come." "We are a free family," I said. "It is our custom to move
about freely and use what we need to use. If something is needed in the refrigerator, juice, ice cubes or meat, then anyone should feel free to enter there. If we do not approve of something, we will tell you but. . . it is very late. We must look to our job tomorrow it will be a busy day."

Maria was the first to leave the group, then Geronimo had moved away quickly, complaining of a headache.

With the Steins on their way home and Amelia upstairs, preparing for bed, I relaxed in the living room alone for several minutes. All was quiet except for Juana who continued her yapping somewhere.

I could hear fast moving footsteps, then Juana rushed into the living room urgently beckoning me to follow her. She made a throat-slitting motion, then hurried away, confident that I would follow on her heels;

When I made no move, she about-faced and returned immediately, this time dropping to her knees and imploring me to come.

I heard Geronimo's heavy footsteps on the stairs, then voices.

I shut the door behind Juana who had slipped away.

In about 15 minutes, the tumult had subsided. Miraculously, all was quiet, so I decided to retire for the night.

As I passed through the kitchen, I could hear only the subdued sound of Juana, singing to herself.

Monday, August 4 The static on the radio woke me at five o'clock.

It seemed like years since I woke up this early.

As I walked into the kitchen, I glanced down into the illuminated basement, irrepressible Juana, attired in a beautiful pink dress was looking up at me.

After breakfast, I removed Carlton's clothes, shoes, earphones and other paraphernalia from the rear seat of his Javelin and checked the gas guage.

I turned on the outdoor lights as the Cubans, all three of them, sleepishly paraded down the west steps to the car.

They each handed me a brown envelope in turn. The I 94's were in order as well as the passports.

In my wallet I carried two phone numbers, Ted's and Mark Spitzer's for references.

Not more than ten miles away from home, my passengers were already in dreamland, succumbing to the early hour and Carlton's high quality stereo music.

We arrived at the Ricca home at 8 a. m. Peppi and Margarita were waiting.

We followed them to the plant, noticing that many cars were leaving the interstate and proceeding in our direction.

About twenty Mexicans were seated at the six tables as we entered. We sat down on the only remaining chairs and proceeded to complete our applications.

Peppi assisted Geronimo and Margarita helped Maria and Juana.

A tall, lean man moved quickly from his office to a stack of papers. He took one application at a time and called out a name through an open door. He performed this ritual repeatedly, inviting each applicant to his office.

At last, he lifted the completed applications of the Cubans, three sheets stapled together, and called out Geronimo's name.

Since Peppi was outside at the time, Margarita and I accompanied Geronimo into the man's tiny office.

"They are Cuban refugees," I said, impressing no one.

Margarita, being a much more unenergetic speaker than I, tried to speak twice but the man ignored it. He was too regimented to be considerate.

"Any shift?" he asked.

"Any shift," I answered for Geronimo.

"Willing to work on Saturdays?"

"Yes."

"Does he have transportation?"

"Yes."

"Can he use a knife?"

"Yes."

I quickly asked about the possibility of housing.

"We don't know about that here."

The man stood at attention at his desk, then left the room ahead of us, moving efficiently, like a computerized robot, to find another application form and call out another name.

Peppi brought us to see a man who was responsible for renting out the white houses. Unfortunately his superior had ordered him not to rent any of the uninhabited dwellings because they were in need of repairs. However, in one week he would be meeting with his boss to work it out, providing he didn't have a wart removed from his foot in the meantime, and couldn't walk.

The rental would be $60 a week, utilities and air conditioning included.

Peppi came to the car and told Geronimo, who came dressed for work, about the housing predicament. If he appeared undaunted by the news, Maria was downcast on hearing it.

Peppi asked us to follow his car into town.

I noticed the name, Fancy Cleaners, as we parked near the front door of the establishment. Peppi got out of the car and began reading several notices posted in the window.

There was no work.

After Margarita conferred with Peppi in Spanish, he returned to me with a sense of renewed faith saying categorically, "they'll get a job because they're refugees."

Ignoring the sign, Peppi, Geronimo and I entered a door where we faced a woman secretary sitting at a desk. The woman, who once worked at the plant, knew Peppi.

After they exchanged old memories I asked, "Is there work here for Cuban refugees?"

The secretary had specific orders: no applications for a week.

We went outside to see Margarita speaking to five, young Mexican men. They too were searching for work.

Peppi and I sat on the curbstone and tossed pebbles across the street.

He thought it informative for me to know of the rumor that anyone who worked at the cleaning place would have less of a chance to be hired by the meat plant. Unfortunately, we didn't have the luxury of being faced with that kind of concern.

Peppi wanted to be certain I had his phone number and asked for mine.

Since we were at a standstill, going absolutely nowhere, this was my chance to ask Peppi about the address of an optical company. The glasses I wore for five years needed a change.

We found the phone directory in a snack shop across the street and, finding the address. Peppi said devotedly, "follow me, I'll take you there."

With Peppi's guidance I easily found the exact street, but only one parking spot.

Peppi drove around the block one time and, on passing by the Javelin, tooted his horn and was off, with he and Margarita waving to us.

I was glad we had exchanged phone numbers. If the meat plant employed Geronimo, Peppi and Margarita could assist him to find an apartment and locate transportation.

Geronimo, Maria and I left the car, but Juana sat unperturbed, glued to one spot. From her torso-twisting agitation and verbal molestations, which kept her trim, she had become in- animate overnight.

The couple and I walked together to the optical shop on the corner. I entered, but they hesitated, turned and started back toward the car.

Afterwards, I went to a restaurant for a cup of coffee and enough caffeine to keep me awake for the return trip.

When I returned to the car Juana, like a piece of upholstery, remained obediently fixed in the rear seat, reading a dictionary.

At a distance, I saw the couple holding hands. They were running toward me.

His chest heaving for breath, his brow beaded with perspiration, Geronimo blurted out two words in Spanish. I understood neither. Then he began unzipping and zipping his blue jeans while Maria pointed at her anatomy, somewhere below her belly button.

I could see they were disgusted with me for my stupidity as I leafed through Juana's dictionary with uncoordinated, trembling fingers. At the same time I tried observing the environs, looking about cautiously to see who might be watching us as Geronimo continued to zip and unzip.

One impulse was to tell him, "don't do that;" the other was to find the meaning of Geronimo's words in a hurry.

The meaning of the first word, "covering, like a plastic sheath", left me stranded. I could not associate it, in any way, with the urgency of the matter at hand.

The second word, "ordinar," wasn't even in the dictionary yet, hearing it over and over, I surmised it was a very key word.

When Geronimo started holding an imaginary hose, as if he were watering my vegetable patch, it hit me.

"Orinal, oh, orinal," I exclaimed with glee.

"Orinal. . . orinal," I said, laughing with the couple as we rushed to the restaurant on the side street.

Past the rows of booths and turning heads I marched the couple to the rear of the. restaurant, then down a flight of stairs.

"Orinal," I pointed, as Geronimo dashed into the men's room with Maria following behind.

"Oh, well. I may as well stand guard until they come out."

To dispel any inference that we were freeloaders by the proprietor, who witnessed the stampede, I bought four peppermints at the counter.

Geronimo declined the candy but Maria, who loved chocolate, accepted.

At the car, the usually self-serving Juana refused the peppermint, dramatically denying her hedonism.

Two Social Security cards had arrived today, but only two, one for Maria and one for Juana.

When I handed Juana her credential, she frowned. By far she preferred her SSI check instead.

Feeling extremely weary, I napped upstairs to the lullaby of Cuban chattering from the kitchen below.

When I awoke, I was alone in the house with Juana. Continuing with her emotional flip flop, she brought me to the television and asked me to turn the knob. With her new-found docility, she would not do it by herself.

In the kitchen she asked for a banana. She wouldn't touch the fruit without permission either.

After an hour and a half, the couple arrived with a quart of ice cream. Geronimo carried the treat to the basement as Maria, jokingly, took me by the arm. Then she placed Juana's arm through mine.

"Juana wants to marry Geronimo herself. She wants Geronimo to have a divorce."

Juana called Maria "wrong" because she was not the jealous type.

She pulled her arm free of mine, wiped the table with the most convenient wiper available, her hand, then laughed nervously.

When Amelia came home Juana told her that she was Miami bound just as soon as she received her SSI money.

Amelia lifted a bottle of geritol from a box, poured some in a tiny plastic cup and gave it to Juana for her anemia. The brown liquid made Juana's face go sour.

Putting the geritol bottle away, Juana gave herself another, quick dose, this time without a trace of malcontent.

Later, Juana was pointing to her groin area and kissing her hand. She referred to the couple as young and wanting to make love, but. she didn't want to watch ... so, she requested that she be allowed to sleep on the living-room couch.

She threw her head back in the chair she was sitting on, closed her eyes, dropped her arms and started to snore.

To Juana's complete delight, I acquiesced. It was a momentous decision because, from that moment on, she would not venture downstairs.

Juana began reminding anybody in sight or out of sight that she was going to Miami but "solo, solo, solo, solo." If she said it more than once, it seemed to get louder with each repetition.

Sitting at the kitchen table, Juana turned her head, cupped her hands next to her mouth, and projected solos in the direction of the basement where all was quiet, but she made no move to take herself down there bodily.

"Clazy, clazy, clazy," Maria sounded off at her mother for no other reason, it seemed, except to experience an aberrant delight. She was pricking her with a needle to see her jump but, ironically, Juana was not repelled. Instead, she followed her around hoping for a change of heart.

It was "clazy, clazy, clazy," over and over, followed by Maria's sadistic laughter.

"Buena," I countered, when I noticed torture being inflicted. Juana's face lit up momentary. Then Maria's, "No, Clazy," just took it all away.

It was "buena" and "clazy" back and forth until Juana decided to lie down, a victim of mental confusion.

Though Juana prepared herself for sleep on the couch upstairs, she spent the first hour loitering near the door leading to the old haunt, downstairs. She was not going down, just hanging around and listening for noises.

Tuesday, August 5 When Amelia and I returned from work, Juana had abandoned her strategic post near the garage, hose in hand. Her weeds were beginning to wilt from lack of care.

Once she approached me this evening to say that Mrs. DeGuzman would help her get to Miami.

Amelia had purchased 25 pounds of rice for the Cubans today. Juana was the first to notice the large bag, stating they were not shopping for themselves because they were accumulating their wealth to go to Miami.

Geronimo had worked alone today without his marital partner.

Juana convinced Maria that having a charleyhorse was a sufficient enough reason to remain in bed and begged Amelia to take her to a doctor immediately.

Geronimo's Social Security card had not arrived today. Hopefully it would come tomorrow. Then we could present it to Ted, the Employment Service and also to Lucille Millner, who requested a copy.

Wednesday, August 6   Salty volunteered to drive the Cubans shopping today because they asked him.

"Go slow," Salty cautioned them.

Nevertheless, they spent $60 of their food-stamp money.

"They would take anything in sight, most of the time not even knowing what food they were taking," observed Salty.

This afternoon it appeared, the newspaper story with a picture of Geronimo holding a cat, Maria, and Juana and myself sitting on the porch of our red, brick house.

I was especially touched by the paragraph where Geronimo is willing to become a soldier to remove Castro from power.

I hurried up town to show Ted the newspaper article which Crystal had retrieved from its hiding place, under Juana's pillow.

He was naturally pleased with the part which mentioned his business. I suspected it had more than a casual appeal to him because, when I told him we had taken a picture of his store front, he immediately agreed to offer the couple $3.50 per hour,

Maria and Juana were both in a friendly, frolicking mood as Geronimo hurried to water the garden.

Juana was demonstrating, for the first time, a great civility by seeking my permission to water the weeds on the opposite side of the house. I was especially surprised at her willingness to respect my refusal.

Maria was in the mood for a swim. I consented to open the pool for her and acquired the gate key from Crystal.

Apparently she did not wish to go swimming alone and asked Juana to accompany her.

Juana turned down the invitation, expelling a excessive number of no, no, no's in the process.

Maria then grasped Juana's hand tightly and gave her a teeth clopping yank. She gave her a few "Juana is clazy" prods but fell short of winning a wholehearted commitment to her wishes.

Dropping Juana's arm in a lurch, Maria dashed downstairs to apply pressure tactics on Geronimo with the same swimming goal in mind. When he refused her invitation she asked me to intervene.

I expeditiously assumed a deaf and dumb role, a policy of non-alignment.

I went outside to the pool site to unlock the gate, as I had promised. What happened after that was anyone's guess.

I heard the noise of the front door shutting and turned to see Juana wearing her pink bathing suit. Her clothing change appeared to be as rapid as her mind transfigurations. Either that or else she had been wearing the swim suit under her dress.

The two Cuban women chattered as they walked barefooted to the entrance of the pool. Though they were only two, they were creating enough commotion for twenty.

Once inside, they walked in a purposeless manner around the pooh They teased each other, with Juana flinging her arms skyward and Maria sternly chastising her for going near the deep part.

"Come here," Maria commanded, calling Juana to the aluminum ladder which was partially submerged, expecting to use her for a guinea pig test. Juana turned, walked halfway to the spot where Maria stood, and bellowed three loud "no's" at her. Then she reversed her stride and walked the other way.

As Maria pulled back, Juana turned and curiously came to the ladder. The first step down was uneventful; so was the second. Then she jerked her foot out as if a piranja bit her yelling, "it's too cold."

Overcome with daring, Maria dipped her hand in the water and placed a droplet on her knee, confirming Juana's finding: it was too cold.

I pointed to the baby pool.

Without hesitation, Juana stepped in. Finding it quite safe, she laid down in the foot of water.

That was the extent of the swimming adventure for the day. The women left, covered with giant towels, prattling as they ambled off, but never walking together.

Later Juana wanted an aspirin for a headache.

Meanwhile, Salty and Vernon invited Geronimo to the ball park to sock the baseball.

He was truly left-handed and a hard hitter, knocking the ball to the center field fence with ease.

Later on, Maria and Geronimo were having a pea soup supper.

Maria approached me with death-bed urgency to help myself to the thick, green substance from a huge pot.

Geronimo rose promptly and went to the basement, returning with a quart of orange pop which he placed gratuitously before me.

The pea soup and the pop before me, I began to relish the significance of the moment. It was treasure-ful. I was being treated like a special guest in my own home.

I opened the bottle, poured from it, and drank, realizing that my gratification was becoming Geronimo's complete reward.

Maria called to Juana in a frantic manner to show her that I was indeed eating the pea soup. She brought the pot over to me and suspended a fresh ladle-full of the soup over my bowl.

Juana entered clapping as she viewed the moon-shot like spectacle.

After supper, Vernon, Salty and Geronimo were kidding around in a run game of baseball.

For a half hour Vernon pitched a ball of tin foil. Salty was batting and Geronimo catching.

"Strike one, strike two, strike three . . . OUT," Geronimo yelled with the aplomb of a professional empire.

Then Salty put his hands to the side of his head indicating that he was tired and the game in the living room ended.

Juana was in bed early, lying on neutral territory, the couch upstairs.

There appeared to be less stress among the Cubans because of the new arrangement.

All was quiet except for the conversation of Crystal, Salty and Vernon visiting in the kitchen, Salty reminding Crystal of her mother's wish to bring Juana for her second blood analysis tomorrow.

Thursday, August 7 Juana wished to return home immediately after her blood letting, remembering the upheaval in the Cuban ranks and the fault finding role of Mrs. Carreras.

It was my unanticipated duty to pick Juana up at Mrs. Carreras' house.

However, realizing this day to be the distribution day for the weekly Interrogator, I decided to hunt for a copy.

I tried the Market and the Mall entrance, the best possible locations, without success.

Because of the favorable impact of the first newspaper article, my impatience to see the second tabloid had multiplied tenfold. It encouraged people to think of America with gratitude and seemed to instill a greater appreciation for our mode of government.

America is a great country and, reaffirming this fact, was a significant way the only refugee Cuban family in South Dakota could serve the citizens of this state and country . . . and I was proud to be a party to that service.

Finally, one hour late, I went to Mrs. Carreras' home and found anxious, expectant Juana ready to run a hundred-meter dash.

Feeling inconvenienced, she felt that one of the children should have been dispatched much earlier to retrieve her.

"The world doesn't spin around you. In Cuba if you go somewhere, you walk," Mrs. Carreras told her.

Juana had a sack containing a dress which Mrs. Carreras purchased for her. But she wanted also a dress for Maria. Her request was denied with the simple explanation that Maria was a big girl and should buy her own clothes.

Mrs. Carreras described the day with Juana as "practically intolerable." Breaking out of her submissive cocoon, she talked incessantly about nothing and imprudently created a scene at the Social Security Office where, beating her chest to redness, she clamored for her SSI money.

The doctor visited would not prescribe a tranquilizer. In his benevolence he called Juana "only a unique character."

Mrs. Carreras continued to believe that Maria was not Juana's daughter. Several new clues surfaced, including information that Maria played with dolls and was still attending grammar school at the time of her departure from Cuba. In effect, if Geronimo had married her, also a question mark, then Maria was twelve years old, Mrs. Carreras conjectured.

Initially it was only speculation, but one definite fact did emerge and verified by Juana, that she gave Maria away to be raised by Geronimo and his father because she was too busy working.

As Mrs. Carreras and I were discussing these matters, Juana was very anxious to leave. She gave as her reason the pains in Maria's legs and the urgency for her to work in her place.

"Is Maria your daughter?" Mrs. Carreras asked, "because you don't even know when she was born."

Juana reminded Mrs. Carreras to look at the papers.

When asked if she would like to spend the night with Mrs. Carreras, Juana laughed and gave her host a cursory hug.

"No, but thank you very much."

We drove home together in relative calm except for one nervous manifestation. One of Juana's fingers was doing the Dance of the Torreodors on her lap.

Arriving home we found Geronimo surrounded by three youngsters, two of mine and one a neighbor's. It was a teasing session and Geronimo's hair was receiving a great deal of attention.

When Vernon matted it down with his palm, he called it a "black rug" and wondered how it would feel to walk through that thick padding barefooted.

The evening was unusually pleasant because there was no bickering.

Juana poured a glass of milk and removed from the refrigerator yesterday's pea soup which had turned into a gel. She was preparing to feed Maria.

I asked Juna that she invite Maria to eat at the table, but she would not hear of such gross child neglect.

When my back was turned, just for a split second, milk, soup and Juana had all vanished.

Juana would occasionally talk to someone down in the basement from the top of the stairs. There was no one below to listen but she talked anyway. Then she turned to Amelia and agreed with herself that Maria and Geronimo should be left alone because they would hug each other.

This day the work force was on duty. Geronimo watered the vegetable garden and helped Salty repair the front storm door. Anna called.

A lady, obviously touched by the newspaper story, would be bringing two scarves for the Cuban women tomorrow.

Crystal had registered one complaint, her blue jeans had white, bleach spots on them.

I had found a plum in the freezer, frozen solid.

Friday, August 8 I again contacted Social Security.

Mark Spitzer knew of the delay of Geronimo's card and had arranged to have it expedited.

While Amelia was at home today, Juana did the furniture polishing. She was far more industrious in the presence of Amelia who apportioned her time.

Amelia called various Spanish-speaking persons for the party tomorrow. Since we knew only a handful with that specific requirement, Amelia decided to invite others as well, including Father Haskill.

Father had a special interest in having the Cuban refugee story appear in the Bishop's Bulletin for the Diocese.

The home climate was relatively calm and peaceful for four consecutive days. Only one legitimate argument transpired when Geronimo protested because Maria was using Crystal's electric hair curler.

The argument, which found Maria raising her voice in defiance, attracted an eavesdropper to the basement entrance.

When Amelia noticed Juana listening to the commotion, she immediately provided her with a broom and assigned her to sweep the front porch.

The sweeping was hardly enjoyable, not when dissention was transpiring between daughter and son-in-law.

Not less than four times did Juana leave her sweeping chore to return to the basement entrance to listen and to gloat, only to discover Amelia guarding that foot-worn spot.

When Maria was off, walking to the store alone, Juana spied her through the kitchen window and grasped her abdomen.

"Maria needs someone to walk with her."

As Juana dashed for the front door, Amelia stopped her with a "no, no, no, no" and a wave of her index finger.

This afternoon the charitable lady who called Anna delivered her gifts, two beautiful, handmade shawls, one for each of the Cuban women.

"I don't want it," was Juana's baboonish response, "I want a dress."

Fortunately the gift bearer did not understand Spanish because Juana's theatrics were mortifying enough.

Except for the playful noises of Salty, Vernon and Geronimo downstairs there was nothing going on.

Suddenly, from her resting place on the couch, Juana yelled out. Amelia, thinking she was dreaming, rushed to her side. She learned that Juana was calling to Maria to come back because she saw her go outside.

She wanted Salty and Vernon to follow her and guard her.

Saturday, August 9   From Amelia I learned that Maria had gone to work alone yesterday. We assumed there was a rift between the couple over the curlers. Also, it did strike me as a sign of marital separation for Maria to be lying in Juana's former bed downstairs.

Fortunately, today we saw no evidence that the dispute between the couple was continuing. They visited uptown, they worked together, and together they appeared under the picnic canopy across the street.

However, in spite of the fact that Amelia reminded them of the picnic twice, they were not ready for it.

At one point Juana said that Maria had a pain and wasn't coming,

Geronimo was playing ball with Vernon and, instead of joining us afterwards, went directly to the house.

Knowing Geronimo's autocratic expectations, it was unlikely that Maria would appear alone at the picnic.

Finally, when 1 went to the house and asked Geronimo to come to the picnic, he did, with Maria.

Both were in elevated spirits and, for much of the time, undividedly visited with Sister Salvador and a young Nicaraguan girl.

Juana joined the group, including Mrs. Carreras, attorney Jensen, Anna and her husband. Sister Nadine, Sister Salvador, one Filipino, one Korean, one Chinese friend, and fifteen children.

She was maintaining her place, keeping a low profile, and speaking sparingly. Like a dedicated martyr, she refused any offers of food but willingly drank some limeade. She was feeling Geronimo's presence and meeting his expectations with a fervid obedience.

I coughed in my juice as Sister Nadine and attorney Jensen endeavored to draw Juana into a casual conversation, dreading that they could touch upon an impressionable topic such as Miami or Social Security. They could unleash a whole lexicon of words which could be ruinous of the reserved image Geronimo wished her to portray.

They thought my anxiety completely unjustified, but neither had endured a post-DeGuzman episode either.

Juana was keenly sensitive to the presence of the uninitiated Sister Salvador, finding it needful to walk with her to her car, speaking expressively.

Before departing, Sister Salvador would hear of Juana's elite circle of acquaintences and her servitude to the Bishop of Havana.

Sister Nadine informed me of her contact with Miami, which I had requested.

Conditions there were very bad, she said. Those Cubans who had failed with their appointed sponsors apparently had the same idea as my Cuban family, to return to Miami . . . and there they were, literally thousands of them, living in squalor under the freeways.

"A year from now they could visit, but only if they have sufficient funds."

There was no word on the whereabouts of Vincente at Fort Chaffee.

The Cubans were industrious people, but they could be easily felled by a charley-horse, a headache or tiredness. Also, by lackadaisically staying at home without notifying their employer in advance could jeopardize their future success as workers.

I was glad that Amelia and Anna had an opportunity to speak correctively to Geronimo and Maria about their work attitudes. It gave me a chance to inform the couple of Ted's intention to increase their pay to $3-50 an hour.

The porcelain soap holder in the green bathroom had been shattered. Juana came up stairs to show me the pieces, blaming Vernon for the breakage.

Vernon began calling the Cubans "Cubies" and Geronimo, a budding practitioner of mimicry, was calling Vernon a "Cubie" right back.

The two were jogging home last night when they heard a loud clap of thunder.

"Shut up," Vernon said, speaking to nature.

"Sut up," Geronirno said, speaking to Vernon.

The subsequent laughter of both mingled with the flashes of lightning.

Sunday, August 10   The visit to church with Juana was very ordinary.

After church we went for milk.

When Juana saw Ted she squeezed his arm flirtatiously and teasingly asked him for work.

She asked Ted for lechi. Ted promptly went to the soaps shelf for a bottle of bleach, a hardly suitable nutrient for the baby.

Maria admitted breaking the soap holder, slipping and accidentally detaching it from the wall.

The day was extraordinarily quiet, Sunday being particularly suitable for togetherness, as Amelia spent time teaching Maria some new English words. Then Amelia's student would spend the afternoon practicing her lesson.

The mothering appetency in Juana could not be denied indefinitely. The propensity to feed someone was stronger than any basement taboo.

Therefore, I was not surprised to see Juana rush downstairs to nourish Geronimo with a couple of hamburgers.

As usual, the kitchen was continuously clean. If a single cup or fork was unclean somewhere, Juana would smell it out. Pouring soap concentrate on it, she would have it over-washed in seconds.

Those dish soaps were being depleted rapidly, even the giant-sized ones.

Juana's secret for energy consumption lay in her halfway actions. Often times she found herself neither here nor there, but halfway here and halfway there.

This evening, pacing on the sidewalk, she decided to practice her halfway skill. She went halfway up town.

On returning, she noticed a neighbor lady sitting near her home. She went over toward the lady, but only half way.

For the third time this evening I discovered Juana standing at the basement entrance. Each time she noticed me she would begin wiping something.

Monday, August 11 At last, Maria's SSI check came in a brown envelope. But there was no sign of Geronimo's Social Security card.

We had six or seven really pleasant, harmonious and easygoing days free of strife. Naturally, I wanted them to continue. But, if I turned over Juana's money, then what would happen? And when she received her check and Geronimo cannot lay claim to the simple Social Security card, then what?

Will Juana rush off to Miami? Will she go to Miami "solo" or will she entice Maria to her side and succeed in taking her along? Will Maria be willing to leave Geronimo for Juana's money?

Just what would happen when I turned over Juana's check? I wondered.

This evening Maria was intent on getting more money from Ted. Instead of the $3-50, Maria's version was that she and Geronimo should be receiving $5.00 an hour.

Amelia called Ted who said that he had given them more money the last Saturday than they had legitimately earned and both had missed two days of work.

Maria, on discussing with Amelia the hours worked this evening, stated that they started working at 5:25 and had worked two hours. Judging by the perceived time the couple returned from work, however, Amelia estimated the time worked to be an hour and a half.

"An hour and a half you worked today."

Faced with the evidence, Maria stood speechless. She stood faultless and uninvolved, as if she instigated nothing at all. She stood blandly but masterfully in the wake of deception.

There she was, legs apart, her hair in curlers, her belly protruding and her arms folded, an exquisite picture of awkwardness, yelling as loudly as she could, "Geronimo, Geronimo."

He was playing ball at the park as Maria made no effort to adjust her noise for the sake of those onlookers who might have thought it to be in poor taste.

Much of the time Maria was using her minutes constructively by writing down words from the Sears catalogue and then trying to match them with the pictures.

This evening I went downstairs to lie down in the TV room, the coolest place in the house.

Geronimo was there and, as was his custom, he vacated his chair, moving to a less conspicuous spot in the room.

Only when he saw I was comfortable, them would he sit down.

He seemed always to be anticipating my wishes.

"At last, I got respect," I said, loud enough for Salty and Vernon to hear.

Though these two younger sons of mine had a quaint way of ignoring these moments. I truly didn't think they went entirely unnoticed.

Tuesday, August 12 Geronimo's Social Security card had arrived.

I was being far less concerned now whether Amelia, who was on duty today, was present or not since the domestic scene was easily manageable.

"Buenas dias," I greeted Juana, who was slightly irritated about something as I entered the house.

"Doaktor, doaktor."

She raised two fingers signifying that her check would be double and it was all hers, not Geronimo's.

"Mi, mi. No Geronimo, I don't know."

Her mannerisms were telling me that Geronimo would be in grave trouble if he should steal her money.

"Policia, policia."

Juana gave me a clear demonstration of handcuffs being snapped on the wrists.

In conversation with Salty and Veronon I could better understand Juana's strange concern for her money.

Geronimo, at Salty's instigation, succeeded in upsetting Juana, she thinking that her money had come and they stole it. They had placed some fake monopoly money in a brown envelope and teased her mischievously.

I tested Juana suggesting to her that, after receiving her money she would be going to Miami. Her response was a surprisingly weak, "solo."

I knew she had sent a letter to the person she identified in Mrs. DeGuzman's Socialite Directory as Maria's godparent and was anxiously awaiting a reply.

When I showed Juana Geronimo's Social Security card I elicited no feeling of satisfaction in her whatsoever.

I tacked the envelope containing the card on the kitchen bulletin board next to several other papers. The first time Juana passed by the board she covered half of the envelope with one of the other papers. When she passed by the second time she arranged it so the entire envelope was covered.

No way would Geronimo guess that his mail was being concealed by a grocery list.

After Geronimo and Maria returned from bathing, they proceeded to the basement.

Juana was strutting about aimlessly, holding a dish cloth in her hand. She made no move to alert Geronimo of the card's presence.

In a few moments the couple ascended the stairs, Geronimo leaving to watch a game at the park.

In spite of a second opportunity there was no acknowledgement by Juana that Geronimo had mail. Even while conversing with her daughter in the front room, Juana refused to divulge any information about the card.

Finally, I told Maria that the card had arrived. Jumping to her feet, a broad smile on her face, she was prepared to race me to its location.

She was bursting with enthusiasm as she followed my steps to the bulletin board where I removed the hidden envelope and handed it to her.

Maria darted outside to share the good news with Geronimo.

Meanwhile, Juana was not only unexcited, she was glum seeing her daughter so ecstatic with joy.

The availability, the possession of the card seemed to give Geronimo a feeling of status as he signed the card proudly.

I suggested that he place it in his wallet and show it to Ted tomorrow.

Wednesday, August 13 Vincente is found. Vincente. Who came to the United States one month earlier than the others, was never moved from Fort Chaffee.

Did I want to sponsor him? I was asked. He wanted to be reunited with his family.

"Of course."

After returning from work at Ted's, Geronimo removed his jeans, donned his blue shorts, white t-shirt and red hat and hastened to the ball park to play ball with Vernon and Salty.

Being skin-different and congenial he was acquiring a fabulous popularity and following among many children. They would encircle him, take pride in sitting with him and admire his batting power.

Geronimo found a lizard at the park and captured it in a bag. With hanky panky on their mind, he and Vernon approached Juana who was watering the ferns on the north side of the garage.

"Iguana, iguana," she screamed, as Geronimo, in his impish frame of mind, watched the creature slide out of the bag.

"Vincente is coming."

Juana acted as if I said nothing. She was expressing the devotion of a mother who would willingly give her male child away as an infant.

The reaction of Geronimo was disappointing. From him I expected a "bueno," at least, or an approving smile. The slightest bit of emotion would have reassured me.

There wasn't any.

Thursday, August 14 Juana was watering the weeds once again, oblivious of the sound of the car as I drove in.

Since she was standing in about an inch of water, I turned the faucet off.

This was the night of the Arts Festival, the night Carlton would be displaying some of his oil paintings.

Amelia gave me enough tickets for all of the Cubans.

It was 7:30 and Geronimo and Maria were not in sight as I glanced up the road toward Ted's place.

Juana, dressed in an orange suit, was ready to enjoy the occasion but would not attend without the couple.

Finally, they were corning.

As they approached me, I reminded them of the Festival and pointed to the blue wagon.

Geronimo, with an entirely different concern showed me Maria's hand. She had cut her finger on the job.

The index finger on Maria's left hand was bandaged tightly, an example of excellent nursing care.

Juana was shocked by the sight of Maria's bandage. She grabbed her head with both hands and began to sway mournfully.

Creating more agony for Juana, Maria yanked at the snug bandage. She tore it with her fingernails, bit at it and pulled at it with an inflamed exuberance as the bandage began to shred and a bright orange liquid began to drip on the tile floor in the hallway.

A vertical cut, about a halt inch in length, came into view.

"Clinico, clinico," Juana screamed as she began pacing on the spacious lawn.

"You see what you've done. You have taken a pregnant girl to work."

A yelling match erupted between Geronimo and Juana.

People were watching the hectic scene from the picnic area.

I looked at my watch and determined we would certainly be tardy for the 8 o'clock program in Spencer.

Juana kept repeating her "no, no, no, no" and moving her finger back and forth in front of her face as I pointed to the wagon while Maria held her bloody finger in her hand, standing in the doorway.

I quickly escorted Maria to the medicine cabinet, washed her finger, and tried patching it with band aids without success.

Glancing at my watch, I grabbed a towel and asked Maria to hold it tightly around her finger and left.

Again I invited Juana to get into the wagon. Again I received an abundance of "no's" with cat-like pacing in the driveway.

Maria opened the door and said something to Juana which caused her to make an immediate about-face. She was ready to go with me to the Arts show.

She pointed to her finger asking, "grande?"

"Silencio." I said, and drove off.

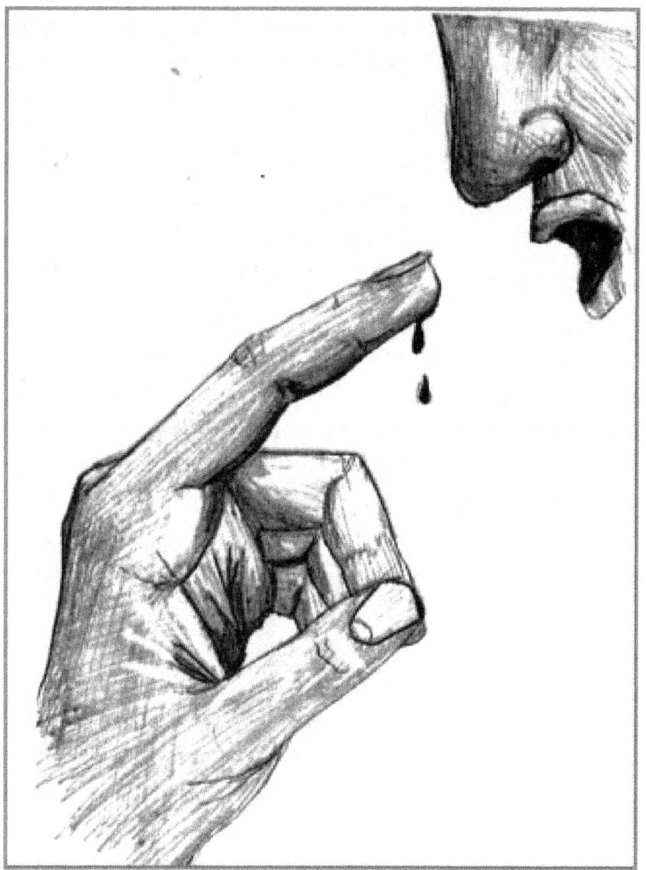

I admired the beautiful paintings, jewelry, ceramics, and string craft at the Festival, hardly aware that the affair was a resounding success. Then fleetingly I had the unpalatable thought of Maria still struggling to contain the blood flow from her finger.

The cheese tasting, especially the pepperoni brand, was delicious in combination with the strawberry punch.

I made a special effort to ask anyone who might be viewing Carlton's paintings about their impressions.

"In two years he'll be a professional."

"The best display of color."

"The best work of all."

I was glad I came to the Festival though Juana followed me around like a lost puppy, pointing here, mimicking there, always striving to give a suave, correct impression to others.

We heard excerpts from the "Robber Bridegroom," from "My Fair Lady" and listened to the song, "The Little Red Schoolhouse," sung be a retired school teacher.

I lost track of Juana momentarily because she found Mrs. Carreras and Anna there and Jennifer, her former employer, of several hours, the one who complained about the flies. Invariably each one got the story of the traumatized finger narrated to them with excruciating animation.

At one point I raised my voice at Juana who was baring the matter of going to Miami to work for a millionaire to a stranger.

Anna graciously consented to have a meeting at our house tomorrow night concerning Juana's SSI money.

Juana and I left for home earlier than I anticipated. When we arrived, Salty, his Boy Scout training in evidence, had bandaged Nona's ringer properly.

I told Salty that Maria's blood appeared to be too thin.

"Maybe they got sugar diabetes from the way they eat sugar," he suggested. Then he tried to remember the term, "hemophiliac."

At the table Geronimo was mocking Maria's reaction when she suffered her finger injury. He screwed up his face in pain and amateurishly imitated her yelling and crying.

Though Maria was intent on refraining from work tomorrow she seemed influenced greatly by Juana's over-concern for her safety. I tried to ameliorate her fear by pointing to the insignificance of a scar on my finger. Then I gave her a pair of rubber gloves that she could wear.

After Geronimo proclaimed how intelligent Vernon, Salty and Carlton were, I told him of his brilliance. Turning to Maria I gave her the same compliment.

For the next fifteen minutes she tried being worthy of the compliment by regurgitating all of the English words Amelia taught her, including counting by 10's to a hundred.

Maria again enjoyed hearing my words of praise for her performance as Juana stood fixed against the wall in the shadows, inconspicuously listening to Maria revel that she and Geronimo were intelligent but Juana was "clazy."

Amelia returned with Carlton's art exhibit.

Though it was past midnight, we replaced some of the wood carvings on the walls of the living room with Carlton's private works of art.

Creating this somber moment, Amelia and I snuggled together and assimilated the depth of feeling in the serenity of each painting and shared a peaceful moment of gratitude.

August 15 As we drove to work together Amelia mentioned that she called a number in Miami, the number acquired from the Socialite Directory by Juana. She discovered it was an old number, no longer in use. Even the area code was obsolete.

We both felt the Cubans were adjusting well.

Except for last night's finger episode we were grateful for the several solid days of excellent camaraderie.

At 5:30 Amelia and I arrived home to find Maria dressed in her pretty green outfit with the butterfly sleeves, standing under the American Elm with all of the couple's belongings, three bags stuffed with clothes, one box and the small suitcase.

They were leaving.

Geronimo was at Ted's, intending to claim his wages for the week.

I was bewildered by events and, seeing Geronimo returning, walked up the sidewalk to greet him.

"Problem? Problem?"

He walked briskly past me.

I caught up to him.

"Problem? Problem?"

He pointed to his leg. It was something Salty did. It appeared as if Salty had shut the door on his leg.

Geronimo and I walked into the house and sat on the couch. I touched his shoulder consolingly as the two women appeared simultaneously, Juana emerging from the kitchen and Maria from the outside.

Some stressful words were being exchanged between Geronimo and Juana. Suddenly, a set of keys flew through the air at Juana and struck the door furiously, inches from where Juana was standing. His mighty, bullish frame of over six feet lunged at his mother-in-law as Maria positioned herself in the doorway, separating both adversaries.

Amelia questioned Geronimo about the problem. His speech was emotional and too rapid for her comprehension.

He was fixated on the back of his trousers with Salty's name on his lips.

I called Anna immediately for an urgent meeting.

Meanwhile, Geronimo was pacing.

He went outside to cool off as I asked Vernon for the details.

"We were playing downstairs in the TV room, mostly throwing a glove around which was disturbing Salty. Then Salty threw the cat at Geronimo, scratching him on the back of his leg."

Salty was reading in his room, keeping a safe distance from the tumult, when I walked in and asked about the happening.

"It wasn't much," he said, and continued to read, not read, not wishing to be drawn into a dialogue.

Meanwhile, Geronimo came into the house. With Maria he went to the kitchen, having just moved their belongings from under the elm to the porch since it was beginning to rain.

I heard scuffling sounds from the kitchen area as I proceeded down from Salty's room. Then a typical Juana shrill resounded throughout the house. I hoped it was only a threat and not a beating.

It seemed like an eternity until Anna and Edward arrived.

I decided we would meet in the front room, away from Carlton's paintings. They represented a peace and serenity I preferred to have undisturbed.

"Ten or fifteen days ago," Geronimo began, "you had authorized that Maria make a phone call. Salty came in, threw the telephone to the floor and motioned to kick Maria but kicked the refrigerator instead.

We withstood that. We didn't complain.

Now, if Salty is civil, he will tell you the truth. He will confirm what we are saying.

Today I was watching television with Maria and playing with Vernon, throwing a glove back and forth. Salty got up furiously. He picked up the cat and swiped me on the leg, the cat's claws scratching my skin. Then Salty punched the door. It is cracked.

I can show my wound to you men.

I cannot stand it in this house anymore because of all of these incidents: the telephone, the scratch which he gave me, which is only miniature . . . but another time he may hit me on the head.

My soul hurts me. that is why I have decided to move from this house immediately."

"You can take us to the authorities," Maria asked, "and we will be at their disposal and, another thing ... if you could call the man for whom we work, he could pay us for the days we worked."

"That kick that Salty gave to the refrigerator; it was meant for Maria. He could have hit her belly and killed my daughter or son . . . that we didn't tell you. We withstood it. Now, I decided to tell you, because he drew blood.

When I cleaned my blood, he looked at me and left,"

"I will make certain that Salty knows how you feel about these things that have happened."

"1 am very pained because nobody has ever laid a hand on me before. 1 am hurt in the sense that no one has ever drawn blood from me.

There have been many things with Salty so, sincerely, my wife and I refuse to be here any longer.

On another occasion, what happens if he has a piece of iron in his hand, or a knife. We must leave now to avoid bigger problems."

"I really don't foresee problems like that, Geronimo."

"Geronimo and I have made this decision. We can't continue living here in good faith after what has happened. Salty has a strong character. Geronimo is more passive. It could be that Salty arouses Geronimo so there could be a very big problem.

Before the cat incident, I was sitting on the sofa eating candy. Without knowing it, 1 threw the paper on the floor and Salty didn't say, 'Maria, please don't throw the paper on the floor.' He raised his voice too much to me.

 . . . and that incident with the telephone. I didn't know how to dial, so I called Salty and he got furious. The telephone is cracked . . . and he kicked the furniture. I was not in the way of the kick, but if I had been, it could have hit my belly.

Even if I have to beg on the streets or sleep on the streets, if I have to give birth on the street, it doesn't matter. I'm not going to stay here.

We left Cuba; we are refugees, but that doesn't mean we have to stand being hurt. We didn't ask to come here.

We haven't given Salty a solitary reason . . ."

"We've been treated real well and correctly by most. The one we've had the family problem with is Juana, and the problem has been between her and us. . . not her and you."

"Where do you want to go?"

"Wherever you want to drop us off? In a police station, Miami, or any place," responded Maria. "Do you want to go to Miami?"

"Yes. wherever you want."

"Not where I want, Maria, where you want."

"Wherever we can find refuge."

"If you go to Miami, and they find you on the street, then they will send you to Ft. Chaffee and you will go to another home."

"Can't we find other sponsors now?"

"It is not that easy to find other sponsors because I am the only sponsor of a Cuban family in this state."

"How about New Jersey?"

"No. Only if people contact the social agency can that be done."

"You can take us to the police station..."

"Well, what can they do for you?"

"We can't tell you where we want to go because we don't have any knowledge of what is available."

Anna turned to Edward and asked, "What would we do in a situation like this?"

"Tell them to stay."

"You can stay at the cafe, if you wish."

"No."

"It is not easy to find a place . . . these are hard times and people will not open their home," Amelia commented.

"I will talk to Salty and see that this does not happen again."

Geronimo did not respond to my overture to rectify the problem.

Maria said confidently, "My mother has a friend in Miami. Yesterday Amelia was talking to one of my mother's friends in Miami. . ."

"That isn't quite true," Amelia interrupted. "I wasn't even able to make contact. It was an old number ... the area code was wrong."

Juana leaped from her chair, went to her purse and picked out several papers from it. Then she showed them to Anna.

"That's the family where my mother worked 20 years," said Maria proudly.

"'Well, I talked to the man at the hospital today about getting a full-time job for Geronimo. It looks promising.

Should I forget about that?"

"Forget about it."

"I will forget about it."

"Now, Geronimo, where do you want to go?"

"Miami."

"Do all three of you want to go to Miami?"

"Yes, I go with Geronimo."

Geronimo asked Juana if she wanted to go to Miami.

"I don't know."

"Yes or no."

"What do I do, Maria?"

"I don't know, Juana, you must tell us."

"I want Maria to tell me what to do."

"No, I'm not going to tell her."

With a final swing of his deformed arm, Geronimo decided, "Juana stays."

"How long is it going to take for the Security to come?" Juana was asking in earnest.

"The Security came. 1 have it upstairs for you."

Her eyes bulged.

"Now do you want to go to Miami?"

"Yes, I want to take a little money so I wouldn't have to beg when I got there."

In a moment Juana was holding her SSI check.

Thank you very much."

Every month you-will be entitled to about $155."

'Can I get it in Miami?"

'Yes."

'We really feel sorry about this," said Geronimo, "but we have to go.

The family problems that we brought with us we don't impose on Salty .. . but he picks on us."

"It will take $97.15 a person to get to Miami one way, by bus."

"When you reach Miami, then what?" Amelia asked.

"Juana will find the family she worked with."

"I tried to get hold of Roaria De La Pesteras DeValdea. There was no telephone number existing."

"I took the number to the Father in church this morning." said Juana.

. .But why? Amelia asked.

"Because he had more time than you . . . and I'm very Catholic and maybe, through the church, she could have been found."

"But I tried four times."

"Mrs. DeGuzman has the address. Because she is Cuban she knows this woman that Juana worked for."

"But the information comes from an older social list," Amelia noted.

"We are still confident that the woman Juana worked for 27 years would help us."

Juana showed Anna the address.

"If you pool all your money, including Juana's, you can manage get to Miami," I estimated.

"If you can call the person we've worked for so we can get the money for this week? . . .

"Let us wait until tomorrow."

"We can go right now to get it," persisted Geronimo.

"But it is late and Ted is closed up."

"To go, yes, we can wait until tomorrow."

"If you feel you can afford the trip, I can call the bus depot and get the bus schedule. Then you may feel free to leave. We will take you there . . . right to the station.

Juana has her check, over $300 . . . that alone will cover all your fares with money to spare."

". . . and we'll pack some food for you so you'll have something to eat on the way," Amelia promised.

There is dress material that is left; this is all yours, Maria."

"1 don't want it."

"I'm scared for them," Anna said. "They get to Miami, then what? There'll be Cubans there and they'll be able to communicate. They'll find someone on the street and, if it is a kindhearted person, they'll get some help," Anna reassured herself.

Then, stunning everyone, Maria said, "Geronimo and I will leave alone and you could find someplace else for Juana to go."

Anna wanted to say something unladylike.

"I thought it was decided, that you would all be going."

"It can't be this way because Juana thinks we want to use her money."

"You are trying to get at my money, Maria, and I know it."

"Juana can leave anytime but not on the same bus."

"How much money do you and Maria have, Geronimo?"

"With what is due us by our employer it is $130."

"What will you do in Miami without Juana? Maria. She is the one who knows where the reference is, the lady in Gables."

"We arc going to make our lives alone."

Anna could see a family feud broiling with Juana saying, "I won't deny anything to my daughter" and Maria replying, "I will live alone with Geronimo."

"Juana, will you give your daughter and Geronimo $70 so that they will have enough money for the trip?"

"I'd rather ask someone on the street, than my mother."

Amelia intervened: "No, you can't do that, no begging, because if you get on the street you can be prosecuted."

"I don't want anything from her; I'd rather beg on the street."

"You will go to jail."

"I never denied my daughter anything. She is my life."

"How can I accept $70 from her now; she told Geronimo she wasn't going to give him any of her money."

"I deny I said it to Geronimo."

"I heard you."

"You lie. You change your story, but you did tell me that."

"I personally heard it," Maria insisted. "It happened when Amelia was going in front of us and Juana was going behind us. It was then that I heard it."

"I'm not going with you because what you want is to take my money. You know how much I have done for you, Maria, I left my good home to come with you."

"She's a mother with many faults. I have known her for 20 years..."

A heavy exchange of words ensued.

"They're fighting now," Anna said.

Geronimo attempted to intervene.

"Then," Anna asked, interrupting the daughter and mother, "how are you going to solve your problem?"

"We want to go."

"But what of Juana."_

"Let Juana go on her own."

"Juana can stay here if she wishes."

"I have suffered a lot with her as a mother. If she comes along with me, I'll never have a life of my own."

"I never denied you anything, my daughter."

"How would you feel if your mother could not get along with your husband and she was always meddling and interfering? How would you feel?"

"She will be the end of my happiness," said Geronimo. There are many things which are happening in my family which you do not know and should not know because they are family matters."

The two Cuban women began talking about sugar . . . the details eluded Anna.

Then Maria said, "Juana wants to dominate us. She had someone in Cuba she preferred over Geronimo. She said I married the wrong man. She told me to let Geronimo go to Miami alone and make his own way. Would you tell that to your daughter? Why is she complaining about Geronimo? She's interfering with my marriage. She wants us to separate, but he loves me. He's good to me and he takes care of me.

To her daughter-in-law, who is bad, she was kind, but Geronimo, who is good, she oppresses. Her daughter-in-law had lived in my mother's house. She never washed the clothes or helped with the housework. It was I or Juana who would do the cleaning."

"She doesn't respect me. Even in this house she has failed to respect me. I am her son-in-law, the husband of her daughter, and do you know what she did? She raised her dress at me. It is a sign of utter contempt for me."

"She would touch her genital area to show Geronimo that he would not boss her around.

I spent 22 years with her, fighting her. She was even worse in Cuba."

"Then why did you bring her?

"I was the only female in the family. I felt sorry for her, so we brought her."

"She had five children, one died. She didn't take care of Vincente. When he was one year old she took him someplace. She didn't raise him. Now he is 24 years old."

"Someone in Ft. Chaffee gave Juana two nerve pills," said Maria, "and that was the only time she was calm. She should have pills now."

"I don't want the pills, I want only to show Geronimo that I don't respect him."

"She shouldn't raise her dress and show her lack of respect for him."

"In this very house she raised her dress to me.

I have gotten up early from bed and have thought to sneak away with Maria. I have even thought of leaving alone, because I can't bear Maria's mother. She has used curse words, strong words."

"The one son Juana liked was cheating on his wife, and that was okay with Juana. Geronimo does not do those things, but she detests him.

"I am capable of making a life for myself and Maria. I am able to do the heaviest type of work and I can take care of both of us."

"Geronimo is the man," said Maria emphatically. "He is the one to be respected and the one the females follow and obey."

"Anything my daughter needs this mother will provide for her."

"I don't want your money.

She's a person who misinterprets words. You tell Juana one thing and it means something else to her. I can't continue with my mother if she doesn't change."

I asked Maria to notice the change in herself. "There was the time when you didn't have the courage to speak up."

"Because I can't stand it any more."

Juana accused Maria for substituting the "sexual bed" for her mother.

She was pacing about.

"Why are you so nervous," I asked?

"I gave my daughter everything; she never had to work."

"What's going to happen now?" Anna asked.

"Juana must realize that she is now 70 years old," said Geronimo. "The United States is different from Cuba, she is acting very independent now, but some day she will be depending on us."

"She is leaving alone and we are leaving alone," insisted Maria.

"When we were planning to leave Cuba, we had to make the plans secretly, but Juana blackmailed us. She threatened to tell every one of our plans. She would scream on the streets our plans so we had to bring her along.

There were some elements in Cuba who would hit on the people who were trying to leave, and that is why it had to be done covertly.

When the Cubans would seek asylum in the Peruvian Embassy, these elements would hit them. I was afraid, because of the fuss she was making, that we would get hit on."

I asked Juana, "What do you want to do?"

"I'm going to that lady in Miami. I know how to take care of myself. The Miami lady will call here within two days."

"When do you want to go to Miami?"

"Someone is bringing a letter. She will send for me."

"What time tomorrow will you make the arrangements for us to leave?" Geronimo asked.

"We don't know yet because we don't know the schedule, I told him. "But how will you get the rest of the money. You will have only $130."

"We want to go anyway," insisted Maria.

"What if you wind up in Ft. Chaffee again?"

"My brother Vincente said there were assaults in Ft. Chaffee."

"That's true, Maria, and Dr. DeGuzman told us if people don't have the means to live in Miami, then they are sent to the Fort, and it is very hard to get sponsors now."

"We can resist going. We can say we won't go to Ft. Chaffee."

"Well, where will you go then?"

"We will go to Miami."

"But the facts are facts. Sister Nadine, who called an agency down in Miami said the situation was very bad there; jobs were impossible and people were living in tents."

"But we have decided to go there."

"Well, if that is your decision, then you must accept any unpleasant consequences. They may be much more painful to bear than the miniature scratches of a cat."

Amelia suggested that we drop them off at the bus depot in Sioux Falls since we were planning a weekend vacation and would be passing through.

The Cuban couple assured us that they would arrive in Miami safely.

"But how will you transfer between the many buses," Amelia asked.

"By asking people, showing the workers at the station our tickets to Miami. That's how we go here," stated Geronimo, "We had to ask people to get here, though we had three airplane changes."

"They'll probably make it," I thought, "But you need 70 more dollars. How will you handle that?"

Anna suggested they work another week and save the $70.

"It won't be a big help because it's only $40 a week more," complained Maria.

"Well, you will still have to find that $70."

"Yes, we can work, and we can work another week," Geronimo decided.

"You can start making arrangements," Maria advised. "By next Saturday we will have the money."

"Would we wait, or should we invest and give them the $70?" I pondered.

Anna was against it.

"But I will go on vacation in three days," I told Anna. "It was essential that the matter be settled very soon."

After some private deliberation between the non-Cubans present I asked Maria: "Don't you want to go someplace else beside Miami?"

"No."

"How about California?"

"No."

"Their mind is made up. There is little we can do. I think if they return to Ft. Chaffee they will stay there a long time."

"At least Maria will have the facilities there to give birth," Anna thought.

"Tomorrow I will make arrangements for you to get to the bus station," I said finally.

Saturday August 16   I was up at seven. I needed time to get new tires before we could make the trip to Sioux Falls.

One way or another, this was the day of departure, the forty second day.

I would drive the couple to the bus depot, give them the extra $70 for their bus fare and then we would be off to the Holiday Inn for the weekend.

But what of Juana? My concern increased when I saw her dozing in her green, Sunday dress, her eyes drooping, sitting on the couch she chose for her bed. She was prepared to challenge anyone who would try leaving her behind.

Two bowls of rice, generously sprinkled with cinnamon were prepared and set on the table.

By 8:30 I had returned to the same unstirred house I left. Juana sat motionless, her eyes staring at the orange carpet at her feet.

I quietly sat down beside her, whispering, 'Juana, solo? Si?" It was like dousing her with a million tiny needles which made her face tighten and her mouth pour out a dozen "No's", producing in her a turmoil which could not be contained. The aimless pacing started, which meant that I could be unleashing a terrible hell in her if she remained "solo."

I was reluctant to tell Amelia that the weekend vacation she looked forward to would have to be scratched for another weekend because Juana would not survive at home alone.

I went to the basement. It was dark in the corner encircled with Amelia's old window drapes.

"Geronimo," I called very quietly. He grunted. The light went on.

I could see one silhouette dressing, then another.

Though it was early. I called Mrs. Carreras and informed her of the problem I anticipated.

"What can I do?"

"Juana will be alone over the weekend; she won't make it,"

"Then bring her here. I'll guest her overnight."

I was relieved. We wouldn't need to cancel our own vacation plans after all. I would simply drop Juana off on our way to the bus depot and Geronimo and Maria could depart for Miami together.

It was Maria who ascended the basement stairs first.

Soon I could hear both women talking in the kitchen. It was normal talk, a quiet conversation.

Maria began running hot water over several pieces of frozen pork chops she had removed from the freezer. She left the water running and carried one of the bowls of rice, Juana's peace offering, downstairs for Geronimo.

I approached Juana whose panic-laden body had, somehow, become tranquilized. "Solo?" I asked, pointing a finger at her. I watched her figit slightly. Then the "no, no, no's" came and her three fingers went straight up.

Cupping my hands and placing them to my mouth, I looked toward the basement and, imitating the old women, I uttered a "solo." I projected a "solo" everywhere. I even opened a drawer and placed a "solo" there.

But Juana brushed off my solo's with a fleeting sham of a smile and an awkward wave of her hand.

Juana wanted dineros from the bank. She brought me the brown envelope 1 handed her last night as Maria looked on approvingly.

Again Juana flashed her three fingers in my face and pointed to Maria's belly.

Juana reasoned that the three of them would appear to be more of a family in Miami. Consequently the police would not be likely to interfere.

Salty, Vernon and Crystal were up busily preparing for the trip when I returned from the bank.

I had placed all of Juana's money in the same, brown envelope and handed it to her. She was quick to place it in her white bag, the one Amelia had bought for her from Penny's, and set it on the table.

I had lost track of the whereabouts of Amelia who had just returned from her usual Saturday morning beauty appointment.

When Amelia provided her with two extra, sizable suitcases, Maria changed her mind about the dress materials. She could take more of what was given freely to her.

The Cubans had gotten into the wagon first, including Juana. There was no fuss, no stressful scenes, no agitation.

Amelia was the last to emerge from the house holding Juana's white purse, the one with the brown envelope, which she had left behind.

The drive was quiet, very quiet.

About midway, we made one stop.

"Orinal?" I asked Geronimo. Only Amelia and I needed to visit the bathroom and none of the Cubans would accept their favorite beverage, a coke.

We arrived at the bus station a half hour before departure time.

The three pieces of luggage they carried would add to their respectability. A tag attached to each with our name and address could tell the authorities that they were not homeless.

As three tickets were being prepared, Geronimo produced the brown envelope which contained Juana's $315 and 17 cents to the penny. Soon it was "all aboard" on Lane four where the bus to Omaha stood,

Maria was tearful. Juana hugged Amelia, Geronimo, saddened, shook our hands.

I was hoping that Salty would make a move of reconciliation with Geronimo. Imbued with plenty of adolescent cockiness, he didn't.

The Cuban trio boarded the bus and moved to the rear, Geronimo looking back and waving slightly. Then Amelia and I, Crystal, Vernon and Salty went to our wagon.

The Cubans would arrive in Miami in two days, Monday at noon.

Friday, August 29   Amelia lifted the phone.

"I got a job, J got a job," the voice cried out.

It was Juana, calling from Miami.

Amelia could hear the cry of a child in the background.

Juana was prompt to inform us that she was working for the Ambassador of Honduras.

Amelia was delighted with the news and asked her how she managed to find work. Apparently, she had taken the newspaper story from South Dakota, including the picture, and walked from one house to another showing this credential for anyone who might be interested.

Her resourcefulness got her a job at the Espinoza home where she was now residing.

Geronimo was not working and he and Maria were living in a hotel.

Tuesday, September 2   Juana called again. She was requesting that Amelia send the beans and rice they had left behind. They were short of food.

Wednesday, September 3   Juana's call was urgent.

Maria had been standing in line all day to register for food stamps. She was in bed bleeding because she has nothing to eat. Did Amelia send the food?

Thursday, September 4 Juana called and was pleading for some money because Maria went to the hospital and Geronimo didn't have the bus fare to visit her.

Friday, September 5 Juana called to confirm that her SSI check, which was forwarded by Amelia, had arrived. She was dissatisfied, however, because she expected to receive two checks.

Monday, September 8 Juana called just as Mr. Espinoza entered the house. She could be overheard telling Mr. Espinoza that it was Amelia who had called.

He came to the phone and, in a friendly, accented tone, asked Amelia if she had called.

"No, Juana called."

"She lies to us."

"It happened to us also, but we would sit down with her and confront her."

Mr. Espinoza didn't mind her calling on the phone; it was her lying he didn't like.

".. . and she blames our 10 year old daughter for her own mistakes."

Mr. Espinoza invited us to visit his home if we were ever in Miami and promised to speak to Juana.

He did not know the whereabouts of Geronimo and Maria but noted that, on the phone. Juana would have bitter arguments with her daughter.

Thursday, October 2 The phone calls had ceased. Juana letter asking if Amelia were sending all of her mail.

She lost her job and was living with the couple.

They were working sporadically, "here and there."

The apartment rent was $285.

The letter was signed. "Maria and Juana."

Monday, November 24   Juana called, reversing charges. Maria had a girl. Her name? Soley.

Wednesday, November 26 "Hello, Gabriel Santorcaz calling, will you accept the charges?"

"Hello, Balthasar Araceli calling, will you accept the charge?"

"Hello, Miguel Borja calling . . . Augusto Centeno . . . Jose Zorillo . . . Benito Goldos . .

"Cuban refugees, anyone?" I reacted painfully.

It appeared that Vincente had generously shared our phone number with everyone at Fort Chaffee.

The End

TO MY REFUGEE MOTHER WHO CALLED ME SWEET.
I LOVINGLY SUBMIT:

SWEET PETE

As far back as 1 recall
Mother called me sweet
Sweet she called me first.
I think, then she called me Pete

To be as sweet as I could be
Became my final destiny
What else, what else could I be
But sweet to everything I see

Are you ready now to come
To join the test to eat?
Not now, not now. I will refrain
I have a parakeet

Are you ready now to come
For juice to quench your thirst?
Not now. not now. I will not come
My parakeet comes tint

You've cleaned his cage
And gave him food
You stroked his neck
And said "be good"

You've groomed his wing
And washed his feet
You've fixed his perch
Sweet Pete, Sweet Pete

You've shooed the flies
And aired the room
And swept the floor with
An old whisk broom

Are you ready
Now Sweet Pete .
To come along
In your bare feet?

You've made no noise
Upon the floor
Now there's nothing,
Nothing more

To sit and watch, to sit and love
Is what I now must live
If ever a person were happy about
It's a person who could give

So "thank you" fifty years ago
To a mother who called me sweet
Sweet she called me first,
I think, then she called me Pete

Affectionately,
Philip Stack

Published by a Self-Publisher

Book List - Contact:
job_elizes@yahoo.com - tatay@usa.com

Writings 1 Book, 2012 + + 1. Obit, *Bambi Harper* + + **2. Speech, UP, 2003,** *Butch Jimenez* + + **3. Speech, Silliman U, 2006,** *Butch Jimenez* + + **4. The Mission Moment,** *Dr. Phil Stack* + + 5. **Subanon Spirits of Rice & Land** - *Noel Cornel Alegre* + + **6. I Look Out The Window** - *Atty. Toto Causing* + + **7. Ride On A Bus, Poem,** *Melanie Ferrer, et al* + + **8. Why Am I Doing This,** *Susie Barbieri* + **9. How To Court A Philippine Lady,** *Rodel Ramos, et al* + + **10. Story of Bacna Surgical Mission,** *Sylvia Salvador* + + **11. Catch That Story**, *Tatay Jobo Elizes*

Writings 2 Book, 2012 + + 1. There Is Hope For The Philippines, *Grace Padaca* + + **2. Pointers On Employment Abroad,** *Melanie Aquino* + + **3. Without KNCHS: (Love story),** *Atty. Toto Causing* + + **4. 422 Years Ago,** *Rodel Rodis* + + **5. Filipino American History Month,** *Rodel Rodis* + + **6. A Need For Reflection, Gloom,** *Cesar Torres* + + **7. Did Ninoy Die For Nothing,** *Joey Concepcion* + + **8. Criteria - American Institute of Philanthropy,** *Charity Guidelines (Feature)* + + **9. Coming Revolution In The Ballot,** *Cesar Lumba* + + **10. 2009, A Retrospective,** *Cesar Lumba* + + **11. Strangers In Our Own Country,** *Casiano Mayor Jr.* + + **12. The Gypsy Soul,** *Casiano Mayor Jr.* + **13. An End To Cheating,** *Sonny Coloma* + + **14. Toward Culture of Giving, Not Having**, *Sonny Coloma* + + **15. 100 Reasons to be Proud as Pinoys,** *Anonymous*

Writings 3A Book, 2012
+ + **1. EPIC25, Emerging Philippines Investors Coalition,** *Norman Madrid* + + **2. Management Ability As An Issue,** *Dr. Rene B. Azurin* + + **3. Do We Really Want To Give Our Politicos More Power**, *Dr.*

Rene B. Azurin + + **4. Will 2010 Fulfill Filipinos High Hopes For Better Life – Metamorphosis,** *Ernie D. Delfin* + + **5. Comelec Is The Root Of All Evils,** *Toto Causing* + + **6. Some Advantages of Federalism and Parliamentary Government For The Philippines,** *Dr. Jose Abueva* + + **7. Sometimes A Great Nation,** *Mar-Vic Cagurangan* + + **8. Great Conspiracy,** *Mar-Vic Cagurangan* + + **9. Of Speech & Life's Riddles,** *Casiano Mayor* + + **10. Bad Start To The Year,** *Rod Garcia* + + **11. A Dinner out,** *Rod Garcia* + + **12. One More Time,** *Roy Gaane* + + **13. Strange Noises –** *Tatay Jobo Elizes* + +

Writings 3B Book, 2012
+ + **1. The Reeds and Beams of Sunset in Paite and Balangaging in Zambales,** *Ceres Busa* + + **2. Memories of your Past,** *Ceres Busa* + + **3. Blowout in the Barrio,** *Ceres Busa* + + **4. Dream on Sari-sari Store Keeper,** *Ceres Busa* + + **5. O Naraniag O Bulan,** *Ceres Busa,* + + **6. Candelaria, O Candelaria,** *Ceres Busa* + + **7. Four P's ... Pastillas, Pilipig, Patupat at Panan,** *Ceres Busa* + + **8. On Being Filipino American,** *John Reyes* + + **9. The Monterey Peninsula,** *John Reyes* + + **10. The Salaza Fiesta,** *John Reyes* + + **11. Salawikain: Filipino Proverbs,** *John Reyes* + + **12. Musikero (The Musician),** *John Reyes* + + **13. Did You Know (1),** *Bert Guiang* + + **14. Did You Know (2),** *Bert Guiang* + + **15. Did You Know (3),** *Bert Guiang* + + **16. Did You Know (4),** *Bert Guiang* + + **17. Did You Know (5),** *Bert Guiang* + + **18. Sharing Trivia,** *Bert Guiang* + +

Writings 4A Book, 2012
+ + **1. The State of Our Nation and Democracy In 2010: Building 'The Good Society" We Want,** *Dr. Jose V. Abueva* + + **2. Assessing the Expanded Role of AFP in Nation Building,** *Col. Dencio (Dennis) Acop, Ret,* + + **3. Assessing RP's Security Strategies, Alternative Views,** *Col. Dencio (Dennis) Acop, Ret.* + **4. The Way We Were,** *Fred Natividad* + + **5. Veterans of Ipo Dam, A Fiction,** *Fred Natividad* + + **6. A Plea,** *Miguel Reyes Reynaldo* + + **7. International Youth Bowling, My Impressions,** *Marjorie Ann Elizes Reyes* + +

Writings 4B Book, 2012
+ + **1. Mi Ultimo Adios (My Last Farewell),** *Dr. Jose P. Rizal* + + **2. Aling Pagibig Sa Tinubuang Bayan,** *Gat. Andres Bonifacio* + + **3. Rekonsilasyun Dula (Reunion in Heaven),** *A Play, Irineo P. Goce (KaPule2 or Leonidas P. Agbayani)* + + **4. Forgery of Rizal Retraction,** *Irineo P. Goce (KaPule2 or Leonidas P. Agbayani)* + + **5. Maikling Kasaysayan Ng Malas Na Bayang Pilipinas,** *Ireneo P. Goce (KaPule2 or Leonidas P. Agbayani)*

Writings 5 Book - "Best Hopes" 2010, About President P-Noy + + **I. The Challenge of a Hundred Days: Believing that Filipinos can,** *Tony Meloto* +

+ II. The 2006 Ramon Magsaysay Award for Community Service, *for Tony Meloto* + + III. Open Letter to Noynoy, *F. Sionil Jose* + + IV. A History of Pain, *Juan L. Mercado* + + V. An Open Letter to Noynoy, *From OFWS* + + VI. Pursuit of Good Governance Advocacies, *Marcelo Tecson* + + VII. A Fervent Prayer for Peace, *Cesar Torres* + + VIII. A History of Betrayal, *Perry Diaz* + + IX. Corona's Thorny Crown, *Perry Diaz* + + X. Dawn of a New Era, *Perry Diaz* + + XI. Of Mice, Boys and Men, *Philip S. Chua, MD* + + XII. A Hopeful Tomorrow - A Balikbayan Insight, *Philip S. Chua, MD* + + XIII. Global Filipinos: A Sleeping Giant, *Philip S. Chua, MD* + + XIV. Heart to Heart - Winds of Change, *Philip S. Chua, MD* + + XV. Growing Old is a Privilege, *Philip S. Chua, MD* + + XVI. Our Cruelty to Mother Earth, *Philip S. Chua, MD* + + XVII. Advice to Grads: "Never Choose Your Heroes Lightly", *Ernie Delfin* + + XVIII. Gawad Kalinga, A Progressive Movement, *Ernie Delfin* + + XIX. Why a Man Must Save and Invest, *Ernie Delfin* + + XX. Beautiful San Francisco, Pinoy Heaven, *Ted Laguatan* + + XXI. The next President and PAMUSA, *Frank Wenceslao* + + XXII. Philippne Budget Deficit, *Frank Wenceslao* + + XXIII. Money Laundering: US Tools vs. Corruption, *Frank Wenceslao* + + XXIV. Amid the Fighting, Clan Rules Maguindanao, *Jaileen F. Jimeno* + + XXV. Why I Publish Writings, *Tatay Jobo Elizes*

Writings 6 Book, 2010 + + I. SONA, State Of Nation Address, English, *Pres. Benigno Aquino III* + + II. SONA, State of Nation Address, Pilipino, *Pres. Benigno Aquino III* + + III. First 100 Days Speech, Pilipino, *Pres. Benigno Aquino III* + + IV. Finally, Another Ramon Magsaysay In The Making, *Bert Guiang.* + + V. A Covenant With Our President, *Tony Meloto* + + VI. From A Grateful Heart, A Thank You Letter, *Tony Meloto* + + VII. The Scent of Hope For The Global Filipino, *Tony Meloto* + + VIII. Fleshing Out The Broad Strokes, *Felicito (Tong) C. Payumo* + + IX. In Search Of Leaders (Part1), *Felicito (Tong) C. Payumo* + + X. In Search of Leaders (Part 2), *Felicito (Tong) C. Payumo* + + XI. A Conspiracy of Dunces, *Cesar Lumba* + + XII. Only Science Can Solve Poverty, *Flor Lacanilao* + + XIII. Education Reform Amid Scarcity, *Flor Lacanilao* + + XIV. Highblood: Obituaries/Reasons, *Flor Lacanilao* + + XV. How Money Works, *Edmund Lao* + XVI. State of Economy & Society, 2002, *Juan Dela Cruz (Txtmania)* + + XVII. Global Filipinos, *Juan Dela Cruz (Txtmania)* + + XVIII. Understanding Poverty, *Juan Dla Cruz (Txtmania)* + + XIX. Kuyakuy, *Dr. Ramon Marquez* + + XX. Cambodian Octopus, *Joey Jamito* + + XXI.

Inspite Of Herself, I Still Love The Philippines, *Joey Jamito* + + **XXII. Love Has Wings,** *Percy Campoamor Cruz* + + **XXIII. Walk For Kris,** *Rod Garcia* + + **XXIV. Coldblooded, But Alive,** *Rod Garcia* + + **XXV. It Takes A Village,** *Rod Garcia* + + **XXVI. Beauty Contest,** *Rod Garcia* + + **XXVII. Eight Points In Enlightening The Elites,** *Orion Perez Dumdum* + + **XXVIII. Case Against "Cellphone Revolution",** *Sarah Raymundo*

Writings 7 Book, 2010 - My Vintage Pics (Biographical) Tatay Jobo Elizes

Writings 8 Book, 2010 + + **I. The Church and the State: In Search of Common Ground,** *Gel Santos Relos* + + **II. President Aquino: "Walang Kaibigan, Walang Kamag-anak",** *Gel Santos Relos* + + **III. What Makes Us "Pinoy",** *Gel Santos Relos* + + **IV. Minsan May Isang Puta (2007),** *Mike Portes* + + **V. Build Our Dream,** *Jose Ma. Montelibano* + + **VI. Hope In Europe,** *Tony Meloto* + + **VII. Wealth in Canada,** *Tony Meloto* + + **VIII. Parenthood: A Sacred Covenant,** *Philip S. Chua* + + **IX. Are We, Humans, Really Civilize? (Or, are we for the birds.),** *Philip S. Chua,* + + **X. Save Our Nation,** *Philip S. Chua* + + **XI. A Time To Pause,** *Philip S. Chua* + + **XII. The Gawad Kalinga Virus,** *Philip S. Chua* + + **XIII. A Marching Order For P-Noy,** *Philip S. Chua* + + **XIV. "Bayan Ko" Bonds,** *Philip S. Chua* + + **XV. P-Noy's First 99 Days,** *Philip S. Chua* + + **XVI. The Practice of Quackery in the Phils,** *Cesar D. Candari* + + **XVII. Remember When? A Brief History of Old and Recent Past,** *Cesar Candari* + + **XVIII. The Philippines Before and What Now?,** *Cesar D. Candari* + + **XIX. The Traffic Problems are Beyond "Wang-Wang",** *Cesar D. Candari* + + **XX. Behind The Gold,** *Eliseo Serina* + + **XXI. May Angal? (Any Complaint?),** *Greg B. Macabenta* + + **XXII. Pagbalik-Tanaw Sa Kapatirang Masoneriya Sa Pilipina,** *Irineo P. Goce* + + **XXIII. Mysteries & Riddles Behind RP's Corridors Of Power,** *Irineo P. Goce* + + **XXIV. Wika - Diwa Ng Lahi, O, Ang Tore ni Babel Sa Pilipinas,** *Irineo P. Goce* + + **XXV. Can There Be Peace; Is There Hope For Progress?,** *Irineo P. Coce* + + **XXVI. Drama Queen,** *Percival Campoamor Cruz* + + **XXVII. Ang Tulay na Kahoy,** *Percival Campoamor Cruz* + + **XXVIII. Sa Alaala ni Maria Lorena Barros,** *Percival Campoamor Cruz* + + **XXIX. Text Game or Text Gambling?,** *Juan dela Cruz* + + **XXX. Of Husbands and Wives,** *Juan dela Cruz* + + **XXXI. It Must Be Love,** *Juan dela Cruz* + + **XXXII. Elite Triad Blocking Reform,** *Demosthenes B. Donato*

Writings 9 Book, April 2011 + + I. Solidarity in Literature W/out Borders, *Simeon Dumdum Jr* + + II. **Macario Sakay Vindicated,** *Gemma Cruz Araneta* + + III. **The Dilemma of the Last Filipino,** *Larry Henares* + + IV. **Ping Joaquin, Fil. Jazz Pianist, my Father,** *Tony Joaquin* + + V. **Bert Del Rosario, Inventor, Sing-Along,** *Tony Joaquin* + + VI. **Xmas Article 2009,** *Allen Gaborro* + + VII. **Beaches (short story),** *Allen Gaborro* + + VIII. **Democracy Versus Discipline,** *Allen Gaborro* + + IX. **Amend the Const. Make Jury Trial,** *Atty. Toto C. Causing* + + X. **Dakdak Beach Resort in Dapitan City,** *Toto C. Causing* + + XI. **So I'm Dark-skinned, Leave Me Alone,** *Mar-Vic Cagurangan* + + XII. **Dig My Sexy Flip Accent, Arizona,** *Mar-Vic Cagurangan* + + XIII. **A Fan Mail From Prison,** *Mar-Vic Cagurangan* + + XIV. **Three Poems: a. Please Don't Let Her Know, b. I Have Memories of My own, c. God Has Made Someone Only For me,** *Emily Espanol Derry* + + XV. **Three Love Poems: a. Some Good Things Never Last b. The Dance c. As I Trod Upon Your Ground,** *Elyn Jean Felarca* + + XVI. **My Advocacy,** *Naysan A. Albaytar* + + XVII. **Feminism: The Great Paradox,** *Laura Wade* + + XVIII. **A Blast From the Past,** *Peter Allan Mariano,* + + XIX. **Bus. Perspective: Bldg. Your Future,** *Peter Allan Mariano* + + XX. **An Overview of Health Connections,** *Peter Allan Mariano* + + XXI. **My Workspace At Home,** *Marge Trajeco-Aberásturi* + + XXII. **Investing on a Home Business,** *Marge Trajeco-Aberasturi* + + XXIII. **A Brighter Day for Little Jane,** *Julia Carreon-Lagoc* + + XXIV. **A Consummation Devoutly to Be Wished,** *Julia C. Lagoc* + + XXV. **No Birds and Beetles and Trees,** *Julia Carreon-Lagoc* + + XXVI. **Ang Wika, Ang Tore Ni Babel Sa Pilipinas,** *Irineo Goce* + + XXVII. **Scattered Thoughts –** *Anonymous*

Writings 10 Book, July, 2011 + + 1. **The Spratlys Are Worth Dying For,** *Ted Laguatan* + + 2. **Ang Siyam Na Buhay ni Felizardo Cabangban,** *Percival Campoamor Cruz* + + 3. **Old Man of the Mound,** *Percival Campoamor Cruz* + + 4. **Walang Kamag-anak Sa Pag-ibig,** *Percival Campoamor Cruz* + + 5. **Congo and the Philippines,** *Allen Gaborro* + + 6. **Divorce In the Philippines,** *Allen Gaborro* + + 7. **RH Production Bill,** *Allen Gaborro* + + 8. **Take the Amazing "Wow! Kay Ganda ng Pilipinas" Challenge,** *Peter Alan Mariano* + + 9. **Your Thoughts,** *MLMunoz* + + 10. **Common Money-Mistakes OFWs Make,** *Alvin T. Tabanag* + + 11. **Don't Just Save, Invest!,** *Alvin T. Tabañag* + + 12. **MRT-3: The Daily Commute Is The Destination,** *Resty Odon* + + 13. **Manila: A Glorious Mismatch, A**

of a **Famous River**, *Cesar D. Candari, MD, FCAP Emeritus* + + **12. Few Filipino-American Nonprofits Getting Political,** *Erwin De Leon* + + **13. Filipino-American Political Invisibility And Community Organizations,** *Erwin De Leon* I+ + **14. I'm 32 and I am still a Virgin,** *Jovelyn Bayubay Revilla* + + **15. Hiding Ill-Gotten Wealth,** *Jobo Elizes*

Writings 13 Book, July 2012 + + **1. From "Criminal" to "Doctor" in Criminal Justice,** *Raymundo E. Narag* + + **2. The Essence of Giving, MLMunoz** + + **3. My Prescription for Spiritual Life,** *Sonja Barbara dL Munoz* + + **4. Anak Ng Prosti,** *Pamela Joy Agtoto* + + **5. Ang Kapangyarihan ng Kanyang Pag-ibig,** *Percival Campoamor Cruz* + + **6. Ang Tato ni Apo Pule,** *Percival Campoamor Cruz* + + **7. Rapture,** *Percival Campoamor Cruz* + + **8. Ang Taong Walang Anino,** *Percival Campoamor Cruz* + + **9. Gender Formula – Boy or Girl,** *Tatay Jobo Elizes* + + **10. The Single,** *Jhackie Eslit Bayobay* + + **11. Why I Am Angry,** *Jhackie Eslit Bayobay,* **12. Rules of Living,** *Jhackie Eslit Bayobay* + + **13. Being Alone,** *Jhackie Eslit Bayobay* + + **14. Love and Hurt,** *Jhackie Eslit Bayobay* + + **15. My First Heart Aches,** *Jhackie Eslit Bayobay* + + **16. Why the Philippines Need Sex Education,** *Reygel Saplad Perales* + +

Timely Writings 14, 2013 + + **1. The Giant Sucking Sound and the Rise of Employnomics,** *Cesar Fernando Lumba* + + **2. UP, College of Bus. Admin. and Cesar E.A. Virata,** *Eugenio Pulmano* + + **3. The Missing Element in Education Reform,** *Late Sec. Jesse Robredo* + + **4. China: Some Observations from My Recent Trip,** *Antonio Nievera* + + **5. Don't invest in stocks if you don't have these,** *Alvin T. Tabanag* + + **6. Creating Your Own Financial Plan,** *Alvin T. Tabanag* + + **7. Anti-Gay Hate Crimes on the Rise in New York City: A Call to the Community**, *Kevin L. Nadal, Ph.D.* + + **8. Native Colonialism & Subjugation,** *Anonymous (TJ Friend)* + + **9. The Way We Were - Fond Look at a Hometown,** *Fred Natividad & Bing Castillo* + + **10. Obituary: Common Sense,** *Anonymous* + + **11. Be The Best Ever,** *Anonymous* + + **12. Remembering Capt. Rene N. Jarque,** *Ellen Tordesillas* + + **13. Why I Left the Military,** *Late Capt. Rene N. Jarque* + + **14. Soldiers In Elections: From Pawns to Knights,** *Late Capt. Rene N. Jarque* + + **15. Reforming The Armed Forces -** *Late Capt. Rene N. Jarque* + +

Solo Authored Books: + + +

Book A, **Turning Points - Empty Dreams,** *Job Elizes Sr,1968 (Renew,2009)*
Book B, **Be Considerate - Behaviour Issues,** *Tatay Jobo Elizes (Jr), 2009*
Book C, **Piglets Unlimited - Wealth Untapped,** *Tatay Jobo Elizes, 2009 + +*
Book D, **Out of the Misty Sea We Must,** *Cesar Lumba, 2010*
Book E, **Fulfilled,** *(By his parents), Gonzales Reynaldo, Editor, 2010*

Dook F - **Reflections** *- Bert Guiang, 2010 + + +*
Book G,   **Writings 7 - My Vintage Pics,** *Tatay Jobo Elizes, 2010 + + +*
Book H, **May Bagwis Ang Pag-ibig,** *Percival C. Cruz + + +*
Book I, **Letters To Matrimony,** *Irineo Perez Coce, Ka Pule2, 2011 + + +*
Book J, **Songs I Wish You Knew,** *Soledad R. Juan, 2011*

Book K, **Make My Day,** *Larry Henares Jr., 1993, Re-issue 2011 + + +*
Book L, **Our Guerrero Family,** *Tatay Jobo Elizes, 2010 + +*
Book M, **Jokes Collection,** *Tatay Jobo Elizes, 2011 + + +*
Book N, **FaveArt 1,** *Tatay Jobo Elizes, 2011 + + +*
Book O, **Beyond idle thoughts,** *MLMunoz, Sept,2011 + +*

Book P, **Cracks In The Armor,** *Mariano Ngan, Oct 2011 + +*
Book Q, **FaveArt 2,** *Tatay Jobo Elizes, 2011 + + +*
Book R, **Balitang Kutsero,** *Perry Diaz, Jan 2012 + + +*
Book S, **FaveArt3,** *Tatay Jobo, 2011 + + +*
Book T, **FaveArt4,** *Tatay Jobo, 2012 + + +*

Book U, **Stack Family Journals,** *Phil & Fe Stack, 2012 + + +*
Book V, **Emily, An Adoption Journey,** *Romerl Elizes, 2012 +*
Book W, **Hermes Alegre Art Gallery,** *TJ & Hermes,* **2012** *+ +*
Book X, **Masaya Din, Malungkot Din,** *Jovelyn Bayubay Revilla,* **2012** *+ + +*
Book Y, **Tiis, Sipag At Tiyaga,** *Raquel Delfin Padilla,* **2012** *+ +*

Book Z, **Until I Meet You,** *Jhackie Eslit Bayobay,* **2012** *+ + +*
Book AA, **Buhay At Pag-ibig,** *Argel Lucero Tamayo, 2012 + +*
Book AB, **Hail to the Second Best,** *Dr. Philip Stack, 2012 + +*
Book AC, **Life Bus,** *Mommy Joyce Pineda-Faulmino, 2012 + +*
Book AD, **My Candid Musings,** *Monette Dioquino Calugay, 2012 + + +*

Book AE, **Tickets to LIfe,** *Maria Lourdes Jesalva, 2012 + + +*

Book AF, **The Dove Files**, *Mike Portes, 2012 + + +*
Book AG, **Nursing Vignettes**, *Jocelyn Cerrudo Sese, 2012 +*
Book AH, **Poor Ba Us,** *R.A. Gubalane, 2012 + + +*
Book AI, **Summer Idyll,** *Avelina Gil, 2012 + +*

Book AJ, **Legacy (Pamana),** *Rachel Astrero, 2012 + +*
Book AK, **Narratives Old & New,** *Avelina J. Gil, 2013 + +*
Book AL, **Buhay Saudi,** *Adele J. Esic, 2013 + +*
Book AM, **Buhay Ofw Atbp,** *Jessica Napat, 2013 + +*
Book AN, **Mga Tula Ng Buhay,** *Angelita C. Esguerra, 2013 +*

Book AO, **Not by Bread Alone,** *Judge Lily Vidallon-Magtolis, 2013 +*
Book AP, **Jokes Collection-2,** *Tatay Jobo Elizes, 2013 + + +*
Book AR, **My Writings Sometimes,** *Tatay Jobo Elizes, 2013*
Book AQ, **Culture Shock, My Cuban Refugee Family,** *Dr. Phil Stack, 2013*

Please buy online or give a gift in paperback or kindle edition. All authors and titles are easy to search, trace or find online. Thanks. Self-Publisher, Tatay Jobo Elizes

All Available at   www.amazon.com,   www.createspace.com

www.ingramcontent.com/pod-product-compliance
Lightning Source LLC
Chambersburg PA
CBHW070017300526
45794CB00001B/344